Training and Development

Training and Development

Prabhjot Kaur
Post-doctoral Fellow,
University Institute of Applied Management Sciences (UIAMS),
Panjab University, Chandigarh

New Century Publications
New Delhi, India

NEW CENTURY PUBLICATIONS
4800 / 24, Bharat Ram Road,
Ansari Road, Daryaganj,
New Delhi - 110 002 (India)

Tel.: 011-2324 7798, 4358 7398, 4101 7798
E-mail: info@newcenturypublications.com
www.newcenturypublications.com

Editorial office:
LG – 7, Aakarshan Bhawan,
4754-57/23, Ansari Road, Daryaganj,
New Delhi – 110 002

Tel.: 011-4356 0919

First Published: **2019**

ISBN: **978-81-7708-495-5**

Published by New Century Publications and printed at Milan Enterprises, New Delhi.

Designs: Patch Creative Unit, New Delhi.

PRINTED IN INDIA

Dedicated to My Family

About the Book

Training is one of the essential operative functions of human resource management. It is a planned and systematic procedure by which non-managerial personnel acquire technical knowledge and skills to perform their present jobs effectively and efficiently. Training is a specialized function and an important sub-system of human resource development. It is a short-term skill development exercise to overcome the gaps between employees and their working environment.

Training may be in the form of learning from seniors, co-operation from peers, and respect and obedience from subordinates. Training bridges the differences between job pre-requisites and an employee's current job specification.

This book is an appropriate contribution in the specialized domain of training and development. It 's catalogued into 12 chapters which provide comprehensive insights into almost every aspect of training and development.

In addition to text-narrative, the book includes short answer type questions, long answer type questions and multiple choice questions (MCQs) at the end of each chapter.

About the Author

Dr. Prabhjot Kaur received her Ph.D. in management from Punjab Technical University, Jalandhar. Currently, she is pursuing post-doctoral research (funded by ICSSR, New Delhi) from University Institute of Applied Management Sciences (UIAMS), Panjab University, Chandigarh.

She has published articles in national and international journals and presented papers at several national and international conferences including Indian Institute of Management (IIM), Lucknow. Her areas of specialization include organizational behaviour, research methodology and human resource management.

Contents

Preface

Traditionally, the term *training* has been used to designate the acquisition of technically-oriented skills of the managerial cadre. Training and skill acquisition is important for every employee in an organization.

Training is one of the essential operative functions of human resource management. It is a planned and systematic procedure by which non-managerial personnel acquire technical knowledge and skills to perform their present jobs effectively and efficiently.

Training is a specialized function and important sub-system of human resource development. It is a short-term skill development exercise to overcome the gaps between employees and their working environment. It may be in the form of learning from seniors, co-operation from peers, and respect and obedience from subordinates. Training bridges the differences between job pre-requisites and an employee's current job specification.

Training is the acquirement of technology which permits employees to accomplish their jobs to certain specific standards.

Presently, working lives of employees are characterized by rapidly changing skill requirements because of growing competitiveness, market globalization, and technological advances in organizational skills.

The main purpose of training is to attain and increase knowledge, skills and attitudes towards work-related tasks. It is presumed as one of the most significant potential motivators which can lead to both short-term and long-term benefits for individuals as well as organizations. Effective training not only develops the employees mentally but also prepares them for healthy lifestyles.

Acknowledgments

I am deeply indebted to many scholars and academicians who made this work possible by giving valuable inputs and suggestions. In particular, I owe a special debt of gratitude to Dr. Monika Aggarwal and Dr. Vivek Mittal who read the original manuscript in detail and gave me many constructive comments.

Chandigarh **Prabhjot Kaur**

1

Meaning and Importance of Training

The value of college education is not the learning of many facts but the training of the mind to think.

—Albert Einstein

1.1 Introduction

Now-a-days, working lives of employees are characterized by rapidıy changing skill requirements because of growing competitiveness, market globalization, and technological advances in organizations. Knowledge and skills of an organization's employees have become increasingly important. Some employees may have previous knowledge and skills while some are new to the job platform. However, both set of employees require some kind of training to acquaint themselves with the job though it is more required for the new ones who have just entered the job market. Excellent employees are the requirements of every organization and large organizations enrol good number of employees every year. Sometimes it is not possible for an organization to recruit trained employees all the time. Such organizations require separate training departments to train employees for undertaking various tasks. Every concern has to arrange some kind of training to prepare the employees for job as training plays an imperative role in improving their performance as well as increasing productivity, and eventually putting the organization in the best position to face competition.

Training is one of the essential operative functions of human resource management. It is a planned and systematic procedure by which non-managerial personnel acquire technical knowledge and skills to perform their present job effectively and efficiently. It is a short-term skill development exercise and planned procedure meant for personnel either to learn their job requirements or to overcome paucities in the performance of an ongoing job. It helps in bringing about positive changes in knowledge, skill, behaviour, attitude, belief and assumption of the employees towards their present job and organization.

Training tries to overcome gaps between employees and major contents of their working environment. It may be in the form of learning from seniors, receiving satisfaction, cooperation from peers, and respect and obeying from the subordinates. It permits employees to actively contribute to providing supportive suggestions on their behalf and conveying it to the concerned management for the betterment of the organization. Therefore, training bridges the differences between job prerequisites and present job specifications.

A few definitions of training are as under:

Dale S. Beach defined training as "an organized procedure by which people learn knowledge and skills for a definite purpose".

Edwin B. Flippo defined training as "the act of increasing the knowledge and skill of an employee for doing a particular job".

Gordon defined training as "the activity which is planned, systematic and results in enhanced level of skill, knowledge and competency that are necessary to perform work effectively".

1.2 Training versus Development

Training is an important part of human resource development, which mainly comprises of training, development and education. Training, development and education serve the same purpose, i.e. 'enhancing employee capability'. Training deals with meeting the present requirements of an organization, whereas education and development deals with future requirements of an organization.

Traditionally, the term training has been used to designate the acquisition of technically-oriented skills by the managerial cadre. However, some other differences between training and development are as follows.

Table 1.1: Differences between Training and Development

Training	Development
Training is a job-oriented process and is professional in nature.	Development is general in nature and strives to inculcate initiative, creativity, enterprise, dedication and loyalty amongst executives.
Training is concerned with specific job skills and behaviour.	Development is concerned with related enhancement of general knowledge and understandings of non-technical organizational functions.
It emphasises on technical and mechanical oriented operations.	It emphasises on theoretical skills and conceptual ideas.
It is generally for non-managers.	It is for managers and executives.
It emphasises on current jobs.	It prepares for future jobs.
It emphasises on short-term achievements.	It emphasises on long-term growth.
It is a one-shot deal.	It may result in personal growth and development.
It may result in improvement of a specific job skill.	It may affect personal growth and development.
It is the result of organizational creativity and hence motivation is extrinsic.	In development, motivation in intrinsic.
There are two types of training, i.e. on the job and off-the job.	No such classification is possible in development.
It is generally compulsory.	It is generally intentional.
Trainees may have no clear awareness of the relationship between learning and career development.	Trainees have experience and knowledge; a clear, direct relationship between self-development and career success.
Evaluation is considered to be essential.	No evaluation is possible.

Source: Janakiram, B., "Training and Development", Biztantra, New Delhi, 2007, p. 6.

1.3 Training versus Education

Education refers to training employees to do different jobs. According to Swami Vivekananda, "education is the manifestation of perfection already in men. Like fire in a piece of flint, knowledge exists in the mind. Suggestion is the friction; which brings it out". Education brings about development in an employee to the fullest extent. Education is a process by which an individual develops skills and gets trained to his nature in a free and uncontrolled environment.

Table 1.2: Differences between Training and Education

Training	Education
Training has a narrow aim to increase knowledge and skill in specific areas.	Education has a much broader aim to develop an individual.
The duration of training is short.	The duration of education is long.
The results of training are quick and apparent.	The results of education are delayed and in-apparent.
Training aims to develop knowledge, skills and attitude, which are needed to perform specific tasks.	Education offers more theoretical and conceptual context, planned to encourage an individual's logical and critical ability.
Training is job-oriented.	Education is person-oriented.
Training is mechanistic in nature, as it emphasises on constant and expectable reactions to customary direction and directions secured by practice and repetition.	Education is organic in nature, as it brings less expected changes in an individual.

1.4 Training and Development Needs of an Organization

At all organizational levels, skills, attitudes and knowledge are required to deliver successful job performances. The starting point and the subsequent steps are represented in 'The Training Cycle' or 'The Systematic Approach to Training and

Development' (Figure 1.1). This is a widely recognized and used model for the processes involved in professional development.

Figure 1.1: The Training Cycle

The need for staff training can be identified in a number of ways, such as during interviews, through feedback from colleagues, by competence or knowledge tests, or from appraisal documents or CVs. Skills and knowledge audits and a SWOT analysis are well-known techniques that can be used for self-assessment as well as for identifying the needs of individuals and groups. This is a good place to point out that while setting any training objectives, we should be using the standard management practice of using SMART objectives.

1.5 Setting Training Objectives

Training objectives outline what an organization is trying to achieve. It is important for managers to get the process of setting objectives right, as inadequately formulated training objectives could direct an individual, team or an organization in wrong direction. Specific and measurable training objectives provide a definition of the success of training. Achievable and realistic training objectives engage and motivate individuals. Time-bound objectives ensure that all stakeholders agree when it is to be achieved.

SMART is an acronym that has been credited to both Peter Drucker (1955) and G.T. Doran (1991). This term is now in common usage among managers who use SMART to set objectives within appraisal and performance management systems.

1.6 Qualities of Training Objectives

1.6.1 Specific: Training objectives relate to a desired state of affairs in the future, and it is important that this desired state of affairs can be defined reasonably precisely. So, the first quality of good objectives is that they should be *specific* in describing what has to be done.

1.6.2 Measurable: The value in having a standard is that an individual, the manager and the organization can see how well the standard is being achieved by monitoring progress. So, an objective should be *measurable* and its achievement should be reasonably verifiable by a third party. This does not eliminate the use of some subjective methods of assessment.

1.6.3 Achievable: Another quality of a good objective is that it should be *achievable*. Meeting objectives should bring about a positive benefit in personal development and job satisfaction, the way jobs are done or in the standards of performance achieved.

1.6.4 Relevant: For an objective to be effective it must also be *relevant* to the goals of the team, project, department and organization and add value within this context.

1.6.5 Time Bound: Any objective must have a deadline by when it is to be achieved. So, an objective must be *time bound.* Communication is fundamental to the success of objective settings. There must be a constant review of what is possible, especially with conflicting demands on resources and changing priorities.

1.7 Factors Influencing Training Programmes

Training programme of an organization is an integral part of human resource development. Obviously, the integral factors influencing the training programmes are the same that determine human resource development. These factors can be broadly classified into two categories, namely, internal factors and external factors.

1.8 Impact of Training on an Organization

The main purpose of training is to attain and increase knowledge, skills and attitudes towards work-related tasks. It is presumed as one of the most significant potential motivator which can lead to both short-term and long-term benefits for individuals as well as organizations. Swanson (2001) studied that less than 5 percent of all training programmes are judged in terms of their financial benefits to an organization. The benefits of training are outlined below:

1. Improves relationship between employer and employee.
2. Reduces supervision, wastage and accidents.
3. Develops inter-personal relations.
4. Increases innovation in strategies, systems, processes and products.
5. Reduces employee turnover and employee absenteeism.
6. Helps create a better company image.
7. Helps keep cost down in areas like production, personnel, marketing, research and development, administration etc.
8. Increases job knowledge and skills at every level of an organization.
9. Helps prepare rules and guidelines for work.
10. Helps improving organizational communication.
11. Helps increasing the productivity and quality of products.
12. Reduces outside consulting costs by utilizing competent internal consultation.
13. Creates an appropriate environment for growth, decision-

making, participation and communication.

14. Helps employees to change as per the competitive environment.
15. Helps handling conflict, stress, burnout and tension in an organizational set up.

1.9 Impact of Training on an Employee

1. Increases job satisfaction and motivation among employees.
2. Helps employees identify organizational goals.
3. Fosters authenticity, openness and trust among employees.
4. Develops a sense of responsibility towards the organization for being competent and knowledgeable.
5. Increases capacity to adopt new technologies, methods and terminologies of the organization.
6. Enhances capability in making better decisions and effective problem solving.
7. Aids in encouraging and satisfying the self-actualization need of an employee.
8. Helps achieve personal goals of an employee.
9. Aids enhancing speaking, writing and listening skills among the employees.
10. Improves interpersonal relationship among employees.
11. Improves group cohesiveness among employees.
12. Builds a good climate for learning, growth and co-ordination.
13. Develops a sense of growth in learning.
14. Helps an employee to handle stress, tension, frustration and conflicts among employees.

1.10 Functions of Training

Training performs the following functions in an organization:

1. **Improved Employee Performance:** An employee who receives the necessary training is able to perform better in his/her job. Training will give employees a greater

understanding of their responsibilities within their role, and in turn helps in confidence building. This confidence will enhance their overall performance and this will only benefit the company.

2. **Improved Employee Satisfaction and Morale:** Investment in training that a company makes is a gesture that employees are valued. Training creates a supportive workplace. Employees may gain access to training they would not have otherwise known about or sought out themselves. Employees who feel appreciated and challenged through training opportunities may feel more satisfactory towards their jobs.
3. **Addressing Weaknesses:** Most employees will have some weaknesses in their workplace skills. A training program allows them to strengthen those skills to further improve. A development program brings all employees to a higher level so they all have similar skills and knowledge. This helps reduce any weak links within the company who rely heavily on others to complete basic work tasks. Providing necessary training creates an overall knowledgeable staff with employees who can replace each other when needed.
4. **Consistency:** A robust training and development program ensures that employees have a consistent experience and background knowledge. Consistency is particularly relevant for a company's basic policies and procedures. All employees need to be aware of the expectations and procedures within the company. Increased efficiencies in processes results in financial gains for the company.
5. **Increased Productivity and Adherence to Quality Standards:** Productivity usually increases when a company implements training courses. Increased efficiency in processes will ensure project success which in turn will improve a company's turnover and potential market share.
6. **Increased Innovation in New Strategies and Products:** Ongoing training of the workforce can encourage creativity. New ideas can emerge as a direct result of

training and development.

7. **Reduced Employee Turnover:** Staff is more likely to feel valued if they are invested in and therefore, less likely to change employers. Training and development is seen as an additional company benefit. Recruitment costs therefore go down due to staff retention.
8. **Enhances Company Reputation and Profile:** Having a strong and successful training strategy helps in developing an employer brand and makes company a prime consideration for graduates and mid-career changers. Training also makes a company more attractive to potential new recruits who seek to improve their skills and the opportunities associated with those new skills.

1.11 Vision, Mission and Plans

An organization has a responsibility for both establishing and protecting the overreaching purpose, fundamental values and ethical principles which govern the activities of an organization. These are often referred to as the vision, mission and values. Organizational vision, mission and values form the foundation of an organization and its planning for future.

1.11.1 Vision: A vision statement is sometimes called a picture of an organization for the future. Organization's vision statement is their inspiration; the framework for all organizational strategic planning. Vision refers to the future of the business, which then provides the purpose. A vision statement is not limited to business organizations and may also be used by non-profit or government entities. Vision questions look like:

- What are our hopes and dreams?
- What problems are we solving for the greater good?
- Who and what are we inspiring to change?

A vision statement promotes growth, both internally and externally. A strong vision helps teams focus on what matters the most for their company. It also invites innovation. A purpose-driven company envisions success as a whole.

A vision statement is a company's road map, indicating both

what the company wants to become and guiding transformational initiatives by setting a defined direction for company's growth. Vision statements undergo minimal revisions during the life of a business, unlike operational goals which may be updated from year-to-year. Vision statements can range in length from short sentences to multiple pages. Vision statements are also formally written and referenced in company documents. The essentials of a good vision statement are as under:

- Concise: can be easily remembered and repeated.
- Clear: defines a prime goal.
- Time horizon: defines a time horizon.
- Future-oriented: describes where the company is going rather than the current state.
- Stable: offers a long-term perspective and is unlikely to be impacted by market or technology changes.
- Challenging: not something that can be easily met and discarded.
- Abstract: general enough to encompass all of the organization's interests and strategic direction.
- Inspiring: motivates employees and is something that employees view as desirable.

A. Functions of a Vision:

- Serves as a foundation for a broader strategic plan.
- Motivates existing employees and attract potential employees by clearly categorizing company's goals and attracting like-minded individuals.
- Focuses on company efforts and facilitates creation of core competencies by directing the company to only focus on strategic opportunities that advances a company's vision.
- Helps companies differentiate between competitors. For example, profit is a common business goal, and vision statements typically describe how a company will become profitable rather than list profit directly as a long-term vision.

11.1.2 Mission: A mission statement is a short statement of an organization's purpose, identifying the goal of its operations: what kind of product or service it provides, its primary customers or market, and its geographical region of operation. Mission refers to what an organization does, the core of the business, and from it comes the objectives and finally, what it takes to reach those objectives. It also shapes a company's culture. Mission statement questions look like:

- What do we do?
- Whom do we serve?
- How do we serve them?

According to Chris Bart, mission statement consists of three essential components:

1. Key market: the target audience.
2. Contribution: the product or service.
3. Distinction: what makes the product unique or why the audience should buy it over another.

A mission statement reflects every facet of a business: the range and nature of the products a company offers, pricing, quality, service, marketplace position, growth potential, use of technology, and relationship with customers, employees, suppliers, competitors and the community.

A. Advantages: The advantages of mission statement are as follow:

1. **Provides Direction:** Mission statement play an important role in helping businesses make better decisions. Without a mission statement providing direction, businesses may struggle when it comes to making decisions and planning for the future. This is why providing direction could be considered one of the most advantageous points of a mission statement.
2. **Clear Purpose:** Having a clear purpose can remove any potential ambiguities that can surround the existence of a business. People who are interested in the progression of the business, such as stakeholders, will want to know that the business is making the right choices and progressing more towards achieving their goals, which will help to remove any doubt the stakeholders may have in the business.

11.1.3 Plans: A plan is typically any diagram or list of steps with timing and resources, used to achieve objectives of an organization. Plans are the written description of future course of actions aimed at achieving specified goal(s) or objective(s) within a specified time frame. Plans commit individuals, departments, organizations, and the resources of each to specific actions for the future. Three major types of plans can help managers achieve their organizational goals: strategic, tactical, and operational. Operational plans lead to achievement of tactical plans, which in turn lead to attainment of strategic plans. In addition to these three types of plans, managers should also develop a contingency plan in case their original plans fail.

- **Operational Plans**: The specific results expected from departments, work groups, and individuals are the operational goals. An operational plan is one that a manager uses to accomplish his or her job responsibilities. Supervisors, team leaders, and facilitators develop operational plans to support tactical plans. Operational plans can be single-use plan or an original plan.
- **Tactical Plans**: A tactical plan is concerned with what the lower level units within each division must do, how they must do it, and who is in charge at each level. Tactics are the means needed to activate a strategy and make it work. Tactical plans are concerned with shorter time frames and narrower scopes than strategic plans. These plans usually span one year or less.
- **Contingency Plans**: Contingency planning involves identifying alternative courses of action that can be implemented if and when the original plan proves inadequate because of changing circumstances.

1.12 Limitations of Training

Training is a basic requirement for enhancing the skills and knowledge of employees in a systematic and objective manner. Though training helps an organization in numerous ways, it has few limitations due to the defects in the planning and execution stage of training that undermines the importance and relevance of a training programme. The limitations of training are as follows:

1. **Time Consuming Process:** Training is a time consuming activity, especially in the absence of a planned, formal training programme with a set of systematic procedure to meet needs for specific skills set.
2. **High Employee Turnover Rate:** Sometimes employees after getting training feel dissatisfied in their job and try to switch to another organization. In this case, the organization bears the loss of investment done in a employee during the training programme. In this sense, training is beneficial for the employees as after getting more skills they start to search for new opportunities in new organizations.
3. **Natural Capability Remains Unexplored:** Training is given for a particular purpose due to which the natural skills of an employee remain unexplored. Hence, they may not be given a chance to share their natural skills and capability which may prove productive to an organization.
4. **Lack of Objectivity:** Only those organizations which believe in strict observance of objectivity in knowledge and skills can succeed in a training programme. In contrast, favouritism and nepotism in knowledge and skills often make a training programme an unsuccessful exercise.
5. **Increase Competition:** Training also develops a feeling of competition and jealousy among organizations. For example, organizations may feel it obligatory to provide training to their employees by observing a training programme of a competitor organization although it may be required or not.
6. **Lack of Knowledge and Awareness:** Training programme by an employee is essentially a self-management process. It requires an employee to be aware of basics requirements of the training programme. However, employees at the lower levels of an organizational hierarchy may not be familiar with the training programme.
7. **Lack of Flexibility:** Many organizations treat training programme as a ritualistic and rigid exercise. They often fail

to consider the uncertainties caused by a training programme. In fact, a dynamic training programme may limit the applicability of the training in uncertain and changing situations.

The dynamic environment in which organizations operate today causes multi-faceted problems that make the task of the management risky and uncertain. The systematic development of managerial talent is one of the primary tasks of any organization and its survival in a dynamic environment. Consequently, human resource training and development is not only an activity that is desirable. But also an effort that an organization must commit resources to, if it is to maintain a viable and knowledgeable workforce.

Training and development of human resources usually helps organizations in increased productivity, heightened morale, reduced costs and greater organizational stability and flexibility to adapt to changing environment. Training and development efforts also help in achieving high standards of quality, building up satisfactory organizational structure, reducing employee dissatisfaction, eliminating needs for constant supervision, and cordial and healthy employment relations through better handling of complaints and grievances.

In the end, it can be concluded that the training of human resources of an organization has assumed a significant role for upgrading and updating the skills of the people and enhancing their competencies into consistently performing assets of excellence.

Points to Remember

1. Training is a specialized and skill development exercise meant for employees either to enhance their job requirements or overcome paucities in the performance of a present job.
2. Training generally develops competencies among employees and improves their job performance.
3. Employee orientation is part of a long-term investment mainly focused on introducing new employees to their new

environment, making new employees feel welcome and comfortable and retain a pool of new and capable employees.

4. The main merits of employee orientation are: (i) establishing clear standards that help reduce disputes and limit liability, (ii) promoting consistent management, (iii) informing new employees of the company's the relevant policies, (iv) demonstrating a commitment to equal treatment of personnel, and (v) providing protection from claims of discrimination and sexual harassment.
5. Apprenticeship is an agreement between a person (an apprentice) who wants to learn new skills and an employer who needs a skilled worker. It is also known as earning while learning.
6. The main merits of apprenticeship are: (a) an apprentice, receives a salary from the employer, (ii) skilled workers are in demand across the nation, (iii) as an apprentice, an employee will have an opportunity to learn high level of skills through personal and on-the-job training from a highly qualified person, (iv) as an apprentice, the skills one learns will not only last a lifetime, they will also open doors to other opportunities. Employees can take advanced training to continue developing their talent and work.
7. Mentoring is a formal or informal process for more experienced workers (mentor and mentee) to share their knowledge about a business or industry to achieve the business goals of an organization and personal goals of an individual.
8. The major benefits of mentoring and coaching are: (a) transfer business knowledge from experienced workers to more junior workers, (b) decrease job turnover by increasing work satisfaction, (c) build morale, pride and job satisfaction by integrating new employees quickly and giving current employees a stake in developing new talent, (d) build skill capacities of employees', (e) facilitate the succession planning process, and (f) to meet equal opportunity goals by effectively integrating disadvantaged groups.

9. The limitations of training include: time consuming process, high employee turnover rate, lack of objectivity, increased competition, lack of knowledge and awareness and lack of flexibility.

Short Answer Type Questions

1. Define training.
2. What is education?
3. Explain development.
4. What is the significance of training?
5. What do you mean by the term SMART.
6. Why organizations need training?
7. What is vision and mission?
8. Define plans.

Long Answer Type Questions

1. Explain the difference between training, development and education?
2. Elaborate the importance and objectives of training.
3. How an organization can set training objectives? What are the qualities of good training objectives?
4. Discuss the various factors influencing a training programme.
5. Why the need of training arises in organizations?
6. What are the potential barriers to a successful training session?
7. How visions are different from missions?
8. Discuss the impacts of training on an organization and an employee.
9. What the functions performed by training in an organization?

Multiple Choice Questions

Q. 1._______ refers to the learning opportunities designed to help employees grow

a. Training
b. Development
c. Education

d. All of the above

Q. 2. How does training and development offer competitive advantage to an organisation?
a. Removing performance deficiencies
b. Deficiency is caused by a lack of ability
c. Individuals have the aptitude and motivation to learn
d. None of the above

Q. 3. Which of the following is a benefit of employee training?
a. Improves morale
b. Helps people identify organizational goals
c. Provides a good climate for learning, growth and co-ordination
d. None of the above

Q. 4.________is the systematic and formal modification of behaviour through learning
a. Training
b. Education
c. Instruction
d. None of the above

Q. 5. Training refers to the process of imparting________skills
a. Specific
b. General
c. Important
d. Overall

Q. 6. Objectives of training should be expressed in
a. Employee behaviour
b. Management desires
c. Needs assessment
d. Subjective judgement

Answer Key

Q.1.	B
Q.2.	A
Q.3.	B
Q.4.	A
Q.5.	A
Q.6.	D

Case Study 1

Mr. Rakesh Sharma is working as a marketing executive in a renowned company planning to launch a new soft drink. His co-workers tell him that market of soft drink is already saturated and our employees are not efficient and trained to deal with the market, but he brushes aside their objections. He has had a sterling record in launching new products. He is confident that he can do the same thing this time around too. He has an efficient HR team, but he does not use its services to learn about his employee's skills and knowledge. Why is Rakesh not seeking and using readily available employee skill database.

2

Training Need Analysis (TNA)

It is time to begin the fundamental analysis of how we got here, what led us here and what we need to do in order to ensure that we are equipped with the best possible intelligence as we face these issues in the future.

—David Kay

2.1 Introduction

Training need analysis particularly plays a vital in today's changing workplace environment as new technologies and flexible working practices are becoming prevalent. Training need analysis (sometimes called TNA) involves systematic planning, analysis and coordination across an organization, to ensure that organizational priorities are taken into account, so that replication of effort is avoided and economies of scale are achieved. Training needs analysis (TNA) deals with the assessment of the training requirements of a target group in terms of number of trainees, their educational and professional background, their present level of competence, and the desired behaviour or skill level acquired at the completion of training. A successful training needs analysis will identify a trainee's potential and the method of training.

TNA is the process of identifying the gap in employee training and related training needs. The role of training analysis is to build a formal bridge between the available design data, the training media and training objectives, in order to facilitate the transfer of training elements into the operational environment. A TNA should always be performed where a major new development in policy, equipment acquisition or procedures are deemed to have potential impact upon the current training regime.

It can be said that training needs assessment is a process of determining if a training need subsists and, if it does, what training is required to fill the gap. TNA seeks to identify accurately the levels of the present situation in the target surveys, interviews, observations, secondary data and workshops. The gap between the present status and desired status may indicate problems that in turn can be translated into a training need.

Training needs analysis identifies training needs of employees and departments in order to help the organization to perform effectively. The aim of training needs analysis is to ensure that training addresses existing problems, is tailored to organizational objectives, and is delivered in an effective and cost-efficient manner. There are three situations that intimate a needs assessment: performance problems, technological advancements, and behavioural changes among employees. However, implementing a training need analysis is not an easy task. The process requires input and cooperation of the top level management and full enthusiasm of the employees to whom training is to be given.

Training needs analysis involves:

- Monitoring current performance of employees by using techniques such as observations, interviews and questionnaires.
- Anticipating future shortfalls or problems pertaining to training of the employees.
- Identifying the potential trainees, method of training required and analyzing how this can best be provided to the employees.

Training need analysis is conducted to identify the training requirements, that is, what areas of knowledge and skills that training needs to accomplish with learners so that employees can meet organizational goals and objectives. A training need analysis deals with questions who, what, when and where but not how, that is, the target audience (who needs to be trained), the task or content (what needs to be taught), and the context or training environment (where and when the training needs to be conducted).

2.2 Definitions of Training Need Analysis

According to **Allison Rossett**, "training need assessment is a systematic effort that we make to gather opinions and ideas from a variety of sources on performance problems or new systems and knowledge".

According to **Kaufman et al.,** "need assessment can be defined as a process of identifying and prioritizing gaps between the current and desired results".

According to **Molenda, Pershing and Reigeluth**, "need assessment can be defined as a method of finding out the nature and extent of performance problems and how they can be solved".

According to **Brinkerhoff and Gill**, "in a broad sense needs assessment can be described as a process for identifying the knowledge and skills necessary for achieving organizational goals".

2.3 Types of Needs Analysis

Needs assessment occurs at three levels viz. organizational, group and individual.

2.3.1 Organizational Analysis: Organizational analysis deals with the study of an organization in terms of its vision, mission, objectives, resource utilization, strengths, weaknesses, growth potential and its environment. It mainly considers "*What is an organization overall trying to accomplish*"? The significant reason being answered by this analysis is, "why a training programme is seen as the recommended solution to a business problem", "what the history of the organization has been with regard to employee training and other management interventions for the training".

2.3.2 Person Analysis: Person analysis deals with potential participants and instructors involved in a training process. In person analysis, employees are trained and changed as per the requirements of an organization. The main question being answered by this analysis is: who will receive the training and their level of existing knowledge on the subject, what is their learning style, and who will conduct the training, do the employees have required skills, are there changes to policies, procedures, software, or equipment that require or necessitate training"? As we know that every job is becoming challenging these days, so there is a need to change knowledge, skills and aptitude as per the requirements of an organization.

2.3.3 Work Analysis/Task Analysis: Task analysis deals the needs of employees who are new to an organization. Every level of the organization needs training in order to increase the knowledge and skills of the employees. Employees at the lower level are generally inexperienced and it is the responsibility of the organization to train them. Work analysis deals with analysis of the job and the requirements for performing the job. It is also known as task analysis or job analysis. This analysis seeks to specify the main duties and skill level required to perform a job. This helps ensure that the training which is developed will include relevant links to the contents of the present job.

2.3.4 Performance Analysis: Performance analysis deals with the employee's actual performance. This analysis mainly considers that if employees are performing up to the established standard performance or not. If the performance is below expectations can training help improve this performance or not. The main purpose of the performance analysis is to check if there exists any performance gap?

2.3.5 Content Analysis: Content analysis deals with the study of documents, laws, and procedures used while performing a job duty. This analysis mainly deals with what knowledge or information is required for this job. This information comes from manuals, documents, or regulations. It is important that the content of the training does not conflict or contradict with the job requirements. An experienced worker can assist, as a subject matter expert in determining the appropriate training material.

2.3.6 Training Suitability Analysis: Training suitability analysis deals with the analysis of whether training is the desired solution for the performance deficiency or not. Training is one of several solutions to employment problems. Nevertheless, it may not always be the best solution. Training will not render competent, those employees who simply do not have the capacity to learn to do a given task.

2.3.7 Cost-Benefit Analysis: Cost-benefit analysis deals with the analysis of return on investment (ROI) of training. Effective training results in a return of value to an organization that is greater than the initial investment to produce or administer training. In cost-benefit analysis, an instructor takes a long hard look at the financial side of training to know whether training makes any economic sense—before we can accurately forecast the cost of training, training methods, the participants and compensation package of people associated with the project.

2.4 Why Do Organizations Conduct Training Need Analysis?

Training need analysis is a systematic effort to determine what caused performance to be less than expected or required. The trigger for training need analysis occurs when actual organizational performance is less than expected. A training need analysis helps to set standard performance levels and KSAs. A TNA gives more than just evaluation process. A good training need analysis not only ensures that only required employees will be given training, but also provide the data to show the significance of the training to the trainees. On the other hand, if it is not appropriately conducted, any one or more of the following conditions might arise:

1. Training programmes may have the wrong content, objectives, or methods.
2. Training may be wrongly used as a solution to a performance problem, especially when the solution should deal with employee motivation, job design, or a better communication.
3. Training may not deliver the expected learning, behavioural change, or financial results that the company expects.
4. Trainees may be given training programmes for which they

do not have the basic skills, prerequisite skills, or confidence needed to learn.

5. Financial expenditures will be done on training programmes that are needless because they are not related to the organizational strategy.

2.5 Who is Responsible to Identify Training Needs?

The main purpose of need analysis is to determine whether a training need occurs, who it occur for, and for what task training is essential. It is very significant to include managers, top level management, trainers, and employees in the need assessment process. Conventionally, only trainers were the major part of the need analysis, but these days, top level management, trainers, managers, and trainees are involved in the need analysis process.

2.5.1 Top Level Management: Top level managers consist of chairman, general managers, managing directors, chief executive officers (CEOs), and vice presidents. Top level management views the needs assessment procedure from a broader perspective. They do not focus on specific jobs. They are involved in the needs assessment process to identify the role of training in relation to other human resource practices in the company and identifying what business functions or units need training (person analysis) and determine if an organization has the knowledge, skills, and capability in the employees that are essential to meet its strategy and be competitive in the marketplace. However, top level management helps to determine if training is related to the company's business strategy, vision, mission, goals or objectives.

2.5.2 Managers: Managers are more concerned with how training may influence the achievement of organizational objectives they supervise. Managers can identify the needs of training by focusing on departmental performance results, individual performance appraisals, future plans, and new equipments and systems. They are involved in need assessment process to identify:

1. How much of the budget they want to devote to training?

2. Methodology to be used to impart training.
3. Types of employees who should receive training.
4. For what jobs training can help in terms of improving products or customer service.

2.5.3 Training Manager: Training managers will be responsible for implementation and monitoring of training needs in an integrated manner and aim for the end result of improved performance within the organization. They should act as an interface between the department and the trainer, trainee and the training division. They are actively involved in the design and delivery of training plans and training programmes, as well as evaluation.

2.5.4 Employees: A training need indicates a shortage of skills or abilities, which could be reduced or eliminated by means of training. Hence, it is important that employees should take initiatives by improving their current performance or to prepare for other jobs. They should develop a good understanding of the knowledge, skills and abilities that an organization will need in the future.

2.6 Training Need Analysis Model

Training need analysis model indicates three types of analysis involved in needs assessment. There are many different constraints that tell that training is important for an organization and the employees. It may include impact of globalization, performance problems, advanced technology, internal or external customer requests for training, job redesign, new legislations, change in customer preferences, new products, or employees' lack of basic skills. The details of the training need analysis model are as follows.

2.6.1 Organizational Analysis: Organizational analysis focuses on strategic planning, business needs and goals. It starts with the assessment of internal environment of an organization such as, procedures, structure, policies, strengths and weaknesses and external environment such as opportunities and threats. After doing the SWOT analysis, weaknesses can be dealt with training interventions, while strengths can be further enhanced with continued training. Threats can be reduced by identifying the areas where training is required. And opportunities can be exploited by balancing it against costs.

Organizational assessment takes into consideration various additional factors, including changing demographics, political trends, technology, and the economy. For this approach, the HR department is required to be involved in strategic planning. In this planning, HR develops strategies to be sure that the employees in an organization have the required knowledge, skills, and attributes (KSAs) based on the future KSA requirements at each level. The organizational analysis should identify environmental impacts, changing work force demographics and the need to address cultural or language barriers, changing technology and automation, increasing global or world market places, political trends such as sexual harassment and workplace violence, organizational goals and resources available and organizational climate for support.

2.6.2 Task Analysis: Task analysis examines the skills, knowledge, and abilities required for to perform a task. It identifies the discrepancies or gaps and examines the new ways to do a job to eliminate discrepancies or gaps. Training need analysis at operational level focuses on the work that is being assigned to the employees. The job analyst collects the information on whether the job is clearly understood by an employee or not. He gathers this information through technical interview, observation, psychological test, and close-ended and open-ended questionnaires. These days, jobs are becoming dynamic and keep changing over time and employees need to prepare for these changes. The job analyst also gathers information on the tasks required to be done plus the tasks that will be required in the future. Based on this information collected, TNA is done.

2.6.3 Individual Analysis: Individual assessment involves how well an employee is doing a job and determines an individual's capacity to do a new or different work. Individual assessment provides information on which employees need training. The information needed to make this decision can come from a variety of sources. Regardless of the sources of information, it is very important to make sure that training is what is needed to address any gaps between an individual's performance and the desired outcomes.

Individual analysis helps to determine employees' readiness for training. Readiness for training indicates whether: (a) employees have the personal characteristics (knowledge, skills, ability, attitudes, beliefs, and motivation) essential to learn programme content and apply it on the job, and (b) working environment will assist learning and not obstruct with the performance. Generally, it is seen that employees who are unhappy at work and not performing well might actually have the right qualifications but not willing to use them. This highlights a key point about individual analysis and training effectiveness. Individual analysis is a great tool to identify situations in which employees simply are not properly trained. When employees are capable but not motivated to perform, performance management is a necessary course of action. In such circumstances, the resources spent to train the person are not likely to result in a high pay-off; they will only increase the training cost.

HR managers should remember that when an employee is not performing well, the problem might not be a lack of skill or lack of motivation. Rather, the manager may not be communicating to the person what the organization's expectations are. Consequently, the employee might not need training but rather might need to have his or her job responsibilities clarified.

2.7 Value of Training Need Assessment to an Organization

Need assessment helps to protect the resources of an organization and assures that resources set aside to address training issues are preserved and used only for that purpose. A need assessment helps to determine whether training is an appropriate solution to a performance deficiency. If training is not increasing an employee's knowledge and skill, then training is inappropriate. Conducting training without its need, purpose and objectives will lead to wastage of funds and resources. Following are the benefits of training need assessment:

1. It helps to identify performance requirements or needs within the organization in order to help in directing resources to the areas of greatest need.
2. It helps the trainer to know about the needs of the trainers for the trainees.
3. It tries to bridge the gap between standard performance and actual performance of the trainees.
4. It is essential to set objectives in order to know how effectively the training has been conducted.
5. It helps improve the productivity of employees.
6. Trainers feel more accountable and more clearly linked to other human resource activities in an organization.
7. It improves the quality of goods and services produced.
8. It helps to fulfil the objectives and goals of the organization.
9. It determines the benchmark for evaluation of training.
10. It increases the motivation of the participants.
11. It reduces the cost and time on training programme.
12. It determines the working environment for training activity.

2.8 Principles of Training Needs Analysis

Planning is integral to a successful TNA and it is important to ensure that a consistent approach is followed when liaising with all potential members of the network. While doing training need analysis, an organization must focus on the following steps:

1. Prepare thoroughly.
2. Follow a structured methodology.
3. Link training needs with the objectives of the organization.
4. Ensure commitment from employees to participate in the TNA.
5. Communicate with all those involved in the TNA.
6. Ensure an organization has the analytical and communication skills to conduct the TNA.
7. Collect the results gathered.

2.9 Processes of TNA

The process of training need analysis can be divided into nine steps:

2.9.1 Determine the Desired Business Outcomes: It is a very important task for the employer to articulate the goals and objectives of training. He must determine that what are the expected business outcomes of training? A training goal should correspond to a business objective. Training and organizational goals should be specific to an individual employee, work unit, department or the entire organization. The ultimate goal of training should be clearly expressed and kept at the forefront to ensure that the entire training needs analysis process maintains the desired outcomes in mind.

2.9.2 Relationship between Desired Business Outcomes and Employee Behaviour: In this step, employers should identify the desired critical competencies, i.e., behaviours and associated knowledge, skills, abilities and personal characteristics that are linked to desired business outcomes. This is so because there are generally multiple behaviours that are associated with any desired business outcome and these behaviours are frequently done by collecting information from subject matter experts. Data collection may take the form of interviews, focus groups or surveys. Despite the method used, the data should result in a clear understanding of how important each competency is in achieving the desired business goal.

2.9.3 Identify Trainable Competencies: Competencies refer to the demonstrable characteristics of a person, including knowledge, skills, efforts, responsibility and working conditions and it is not an easy task to improve the competencies. So, it may be more effective for an organization to recruit employees with specialized knowledge and skills than to educate and train them. Organizations should evaluate each critical competency and determine if each one is something they expect employees to possess prior to their entry in an organization. Hence, this should provide employers with a list of critical competencies that are amenable to training.

2.9.4 Evaluate Competencies: It is a very critical step in the TNA process where employers should determine the extent to which their employees possess competencies. In this regard, performance evaluation surveys are best used to evaluate observable behaviours of the employees. This can be easily accomplished by underlining the critical competencies and having knowledgeable people rate the targeted employees' behaviours. Most often, supervisors perform this function. However, multiple raters, including peers, subordinates and customers, are often used to evaluate the performance evaluation of supervisors and executives. This approach is generally known as 360 degree surveys.

Performance evaluation surveys have become less effective as raters have to gather unobservable competencies such as ability, skills and personality. Evaluation of these competencies is better accomplished through the use of professional tests and assessments. There are many tests available in the market to measure specific skills, abilities and personality characteristics. However, choosing the right test should be done in coordination with a reputed psychologist. Proper care should be taken in selecting tests that are valid measures of the targeted competency. Custom-designed assessments are also considered appropriate, especially if the employer desires to measure specialized knowledge or effectiveness in a major segment of the work. These can range from multiple choice job knowledge tests to elaborate job simulations. For example, a very effective approach to measuring the training needs of supervisors and leaders is using an assessment centre, which is comprised of different role-play exercises that parallel managerial situations.

2.9.5 Determine Performance Gaps: In this step, individual results are combined to assess how many employees are in need of improvement in particular competencies. For this, the employer first needs to establish what comprises a performance gap—this standard will vary from employer to employer. Setting standards will provide the employer with an understanding of how many employees fall above or below that standard. Those falling below would be considered to be in need of training.

2.9.6 Prioritize Training Needs: This is a critical phase of the TNA process. In this, all the information collected must be analyzed to identify training needs. In this, organization should total how many or what percentage of the targeted workforce needs training. Employers should also consider the importance of competency while setting the objectives of training. The use of problem solving techniques during the TNA will assist in the regard.

2.9.7 Determine the Method to Train: After setting the objectives of training, employers should consider how best to train their workforce. Typical training methods include on the job training methods and off the job training methods. It is suggested that organizations should consult a professional who is well versed to help an organization in determining the best ways by which employees can acquire a particular competency. Some learning methods will work better than others. Although no two people learn or retain same information in the same way, studies show that individuals retain information much better if they actually perform a skill or a task. It will lead to 75 percent retention of skill in an employee as compared to lecture, where retention is only 5 percent. Organizations should keep this in mind and strive for the training method that will not only be suitable for the material, but also have the best chance for retention by employees.

2.9.8 Conduct a Cost-Benefit Analysis: In this step, employers need to consider the costs and benefits associated with a particular training method and the extent to which performance gaps can be combined into the same training experience. Cost of training includes:

1. Training time.
2. Training content development if designed in-house.
3. Training evaluation and acquisition if purchased from vendor.
4. Training content delivery.

5. Travel and logistical expenses.

Different training methods will have varying degrees of effectiveness. For instance, while web-based training may be the least costly, this may not be the best way for employees to deve!op a particular skill. Employers need to strike a balance between the cost of a particular training method and its ability to achieve the desired results.

2.9.9 Planning for Training Evaluation: The last step in TNA process is to determine the effectiveness of the training programme. Training is only effective if the material is retained and used on the job.

2.10 Methods to Identify Training Needs

There are many methods, which can be used to assemble information for identifying training needs. These methods basically fall into three categories: interviews, questionnaires, and meetings. Interviews are usually procedures used with individuals. Questionnaires and meetings are used with larger groups of people. Interviews and meetings are in-person information-gathering procedures. Questionnaires are most often handled through some type of mail, email, or fax distribution although sometimes they are completed in meetings. Each type of procedure has its advantages and disadvantages, and each tends to lend itself better to certain situations than to others. Often to improve results, involve large groups in the process, and improve reliability of the collected information, more than one procedure is used to collect information in an investigation. Each method works in given circumstances; therefore, organizations must determine which one is the best for them. None of these methods can stand alone. Always use at least two, if for no other reason to validate their findings.

2.10.1 Individual Procedures: Individual training needs analysis procedures are one-on-one methods. They involve the information gatherer, the information provider and primarily use oral communication. The ones most typically used are interviews and performance reviews. However, there are a number of varieties within these two techniques. These are described below along with several other sources of information that can assist in a training needs analysis.

1. **Interviews:** The use of interviews in conducting the needs analysis is strongly recommended. The interview is a one-on-one, in-person, planned, and structured meeting. It is designed and conducted for the specific purpose of obtaining the required information. Interviews are generally used when there are relatively few (sometimes only one) persons from whom to obtain information.
2. **Panel Interviews:** A panel interview, also known as board interview, comprises of a team of interviewers (usually two or three), who together interview each candidate at the same time; in the same room and then combine their scores into a final panel score.
3. **Phone Interviews**: These days, employers have started to conduct an interview by telephone. These can be more reliable than face to face interviews for judging an interviewee's intellect, interpersonal skill and conscientiousness. Because neither applicant needs concern about things like appearance, so each participant focuses on substantive answers.
4. **Video Interviews:** Organizations have used web to do selection interviews (particularly the preliminary and pre-screening interviews) and with the widespread use of Skype type products. The use of video interviews is growing day by day. The IITs and IIMs use video interviews to select faculty members from outside India. The process includes not only an interview with the expert panel, but also a research seminar by the prospective faculty. In this method, applicants access web cams on their laptops or PCs.
5. **Computerized Interviews:** A computerized interview is one in which a job candidate's verbal and computerized responds are obtained in response to computerized oral, visual or oral questions. Most computerized interviews present the applicant with a series of questions regarding his or her

background, experience, skill, knowledge and attitude that relate to the job for which the applicant has applied. Some computerized interviews confront participants with realistic scenarios to which they must respond. Typical computerized interviews present questions in a multiple choice format, one at a time. The applicant has to respond to the questions on the screen by pressing a key.

6. **Performance Reviews:** Performance reviews are the best and most used sources of information for identifying the training needs of individual employees. They are evaluation of an individual employee's performance for a specific period of time. Most often, performance reviews are conducted by an employee's direct supervisor on a monthly, quarterly, or annual basis. When based on some type of objective criteria, they provide accurate information of the employee's job performance. They identify areas in which an employee is performing well and areas in which an employee requires improvement. When there is an objective, measurable description of desired results, and actual results are collected over a specified period of time and compared with the desired results, any differences are quickly identified in measurable terms. These differences are called performance gaps, and when actual performance is less than the desired performance, the gaps reflect the training needs of the employees.
7. **Job Analysis Grid:** Job analysis grid is another structured interview process. It was developed from behavioural analysis techniques and is used when the interviewer wants to collect information without the subject contaminating it. In this method, a supervisor tells an interviewer what he/she believes the organization wants to hear or what makes her look good rather than the truth, or an employee may describe job requirements in terms of his abilities rather than what is necessary for the job. The job analysis grid technique limits such contamination. Job analysis grid has an ability to produce information that is free of any attempt, conscious or

unconscious, to control it.

8. **Job Analysis:** Job analysis is a formal process of identifying the specific requirements of a job—the qualifications, skills, and competencies. Such information is valuable for comparing an employee's qualifications to job requirements. It is also the first step in designing tests and other assessment devices. Actually, some of the previously mentioned information-gathering techniques are often used for this purpose. However, there are specific job analysis structured interviews and questionnaires. Other techniques such as task analysis and job sampling can also be used. Generally, job analysis does not identify training needs. Its focus is what is required for a job rather than what an employee needs. Job analysis often includes task analysis or job sampling.
9. **Task Analysis:** It is an important step in identifying job requirements by determining the activities to be performed. Task analysis is a form of job analysis. It identifies through observation, testing, or sampling the tasks and sub-tasks of a job. For an effective task analysis, it needs a successful and trained observer.

2.10.2 Group Procedures: The most frequently used group procedure is meeting. However, there are a variety of meeting types:

1. **Conference:** Conference refers to a meeting of individuals, generally with similar interests, experience, or knowledge, to exchange and provide information under the direction of a facilitator.
2. **Focus Group:** Focus group is a relatively small meeting involving generally six to twelve participants convened for a specific purpose under the direction of a facilitator.
3. **Classroom:** Classroom meeting involves a group that is assembled to receive information from a lecturer, teacher, or content-based media.
4. **Workshop:** This is a meeting generally used to develop skill or common understanding through some type of application.
5. **Written Procedures:** Written procedures refer to any

method which primarily deals with written responses. The most popular method of written procedure is questionnaire. However, tests, assessments, self-reports, and succession plans can also provide valuable information for identifying training needs, but in today's electronic age, email can replace traditional paper-and-pencil approaches. The main advantage of written procedures is that they can be used with a large number of people at many different locations without the necessity of bringing them together. They also demand relatively little time of the information gatherer. But they also have few disadvantages and those are the responses of the respondents that cannot be kept confidential. They are easily ignored, and they demand a structure that reduces their flexibility. Also, many people tend to hedge when they have to communicate in writing.

2.10.3 Other Procedures: There are several other procedures that are valuable for obtaining information. They include the use of experts, combination methods, and other specially developed techniques:

1. **Experts:** External expert, who has specific procedures for obtaining information is another possibility. These individuals tend to be used with highly technical subjects or when the internal personnel are not available. If the subject is controversial, experts may serve a purpose of neutral information collectors. Their great advantage lies in their experience in gaining such information. They are able to do this quickly and with a great degree of accuracy. Their primary disadvantage can be their high cost.
2. **Specialized Techniques:** There are many other procedures and measures for obtaining information. Some may be internally developed and others can be available from external sources. Some may be variations on procedures reviewed, and others may be unique. They may be applicable to use, but before considering, an organization needs to ensure that they accomplish what they claim, and that they are valid, reliable, and cost-effective.

3. **Combinations:** This method proves advantageous by combining procedures. For example, an interview can be used to identify possible training needs, a meeting to expand on the information for the interview, and a questionnaire to provide an opportunity for all appropriate personnel to participate and contribute.

2.11 Benefits of Training Needs Analysis

Training must be relevant to the employees to meet their needs while simultaneously enhancing their skills to perform the present job. While conducting an extensive TNA for an organization and delivering training to meet the requirements of organizational employees, companies can experience a variety of benefits such as improved profitability, lower staffing costs, production improvements and staff development. TNA helps organizations to place focus on the collective needs identified by employees that add value and impact to their competitiveness. TNA serves the following advantages to an organization:

1. It helps to identify the performance goals and the knowledge, skills and abilities needed by a company's workforce to achieve those goals.
2. It helps an organization to identify the gaps in training provision in different department and levels.
3. It addresses resources needed to fulfil the organizational mission, improve productivity, and provide quality products and services.

Points to Remember

1. The purpose of a training needs assessment is to identify performance requirements or needs within an organization in order to help direct resources to the areas of greatest need, those that closely relate to fulfilling the organizational goals and objectives, improving productivity and providing quality products and services.
2. Managers, employees, and external consultants are responsible to identify the training needs.

3. Inferior quality production, high labour turnover, constraint on business development, pressure on job evaluation schemes, career development, payment system, high training costs, high recruitment costs are the consequences of an ineffective training need assessment.
4. Training need analysis generally follows a step by step process that includes determining the desired business outcomes, relationship between desired business outcomes and employee behaviour, identify trainable competencies, evaluate competencies, determine performance gaps, prioritize training needs, determine methods to train, conduct a cost-benefit analysis, and planning for training evaluation.
5. There are seven types of needs analysis, namely, organizational analysis, person analysis, work analysis/task analysis, performance analysis, content analysis, training suitability analysis and cost-benefit analysis.
6. There are four methods for analyzing a training need and those are: individual procedures, group procedures, written procedures and other procedures.
7. Individual training need analysis procedures are one-to-one methods, which includes interview, performance review, job analysis grid, job analysis, task analysis and job sampling.
8. Group procedure refers to the meeting of two or more individuals, which includes conference, focus group, classroom, workshop, and teleconference.
9. Written procedures refer to any method which primarily deals with written responses. The most popular methods of written procedures are information gathering questionnaire, behavioural questionnaire, survey, online questionnaire, self-report, tests, assessment, and 360-degree review.
10. There are several other procedures that are valuable for obtaining information and those are experts, specialized techniques and combination.

Short Answer Type Questions

1. Define training need analysis and highlight the importance of

training need analysis.
2. Why training need analysis is important for any organization?
3. Describe organizational analysis.
4. Why individual assessment is relevant in an organization?
5. What is interview?
6. What is questionnaire?
7. What is a cost-benefit analysis?

Long Answer Type Questions

1. Discuss the principles to be considered while conducting an effective training needs analysis.
2. Write down various benefits of a training needs analysis.
3. How training need assessment is valuable to an organization?
4. Discuss the different types of needs analysis.
5. Write down the stages of training needs analysis.
6. Enlist various methods to conduct a training needs analysis.
7. Discuss various parties responsible to conduct the training need analysis in an organization.

Multiple Choice Questions

Q. 1. Needs assessment should consider everything excluding
a. The person
b. Supervisor input
c. Changes in external environment
d. Training objectives

Q. 2. Inputs from which phase of training act as a stimulator for training design
a. Training plan
b. Training needs analysis
c. Learning theories
d. None of the above

Q. 3. Training design does not include which of the following decisions
a. Methods of training

b. Time allotted for training
c. Task analysis
d. How many trainees to train at a time

Q. 4. A good training objective does not include which of the following
a. Training room
b. Desired outcome
c. Conditions
d. Standards

Q. 5. Spiral model takes inputs from which two sources
a. Employee and employer
b. Employer and government bodies
c. Government bodies and economic indicators
d. Work organization and training organization

Q. 6. The first phase of spiral training is also referred to as
a. Communication phase
b. Expectations and motivation phase
c. Planning phase
d. Transfer of training phase

Q. 7. The second phase of spiral training focuses on
a. Training activity
b. Establishing of training needs
c. Selection of participants
d. Organizational support

Q.8. Development provides_______and_______which helps employees in higher positions
a. General knowledge, specific skills
b. General knowledge, behaviour
c. General knowledge, attitudes
d. Specific skills, attitudes

Q. 9. Which of the following is not a method of individual training need identification?

a. Attitude survey
b. Work sample
c. Exit interview
d. Interview

Q. 10. Which of the following organizational factors affect training?

a. Culture of the organization
b. Learning climate of the organization
c. Market share of the organization
d. USP of the organization

Q. 11. Training is part of which system to measure best practices benchmarks

a. Performance Management
b. Performance appraisal
c. Compensation management
d. Operations management

Q. 12. Organization's training needs will create

a. Motivational issues
b. Faulty equipment
c. Knowledge workers
d. Performance gap

Q. 13. When should an organization conduct training needs analysis

a. When communicates a new vision
b. When communicates a legal concern
c. When profits are dipping
d. When a team requires team-building skills

Q. 14. What initiates/triggers a training needs analysis

a. Performance problem

b. Sexual harassment
c. Setting organizational goals
d. High attrition rate

Q. 15. A proactive training needs analysis focuses on
a. Current issues in the organization
b. Specific performance problem
c. Anticipated performance problems
d. Loss of production

Q. 16. Which of the following is not a part of training needs assessment?
a. Operational analysis
b. Organizational analysis
c. Person analysis
d. Problem analysis

Q. 17. Examination of mission and strategies of an organization
a. Assists in resource allocation for training
b. Assists the analyst place the training in a particular context
c. Reinforce openness and trust in training
d. Assists in creating a learning environment for training

Q. 18. Organizational environment consists of all the structures except
a. Organizational capital structure
b. Organizational work flow
c. Division of labour
d. Organizational reward system

Q. 19. Operational analysis is also known as
a. Employee analysis
b. Employer analysis
c. Task analysis
d. Data analysis

Q. 20. Person analysis determines
a. Incumbents not meeting performance requirements
b. Expected behaviour required to perform the job
c. Various tasks performed on the job
d. KSA required for the job

Q. 21. Which of the following is not an organizational constraint for training?
a. Trainees' variation in experience
b. Trainee's variation in ability
c. Training in action
d. Short lead time

Q. 22. Which is an important part of setting objectives of training?
a. Organizational goals
b. Training needs analysis
c. Employee motivation
d. Training budget

Q. 23. A good objective does not include which of the following
a. Desired outcome
b. Conditions for desired outcome
c. Standards set for learning
d. Feedback for employee training

Q. 24. How does training and development offer competitive advantages to an organization?
a. Removing performance deficiencies
b. Deficiency is caused by a lack of ability
c. Individuals have the aptitude and motivation to learn
d. None of the above

Answer Key

Q.1.	D	Q.13.	C
Q.2.	B	Q.14.	A

Q.3.	C	Q.15.	C
Q.4.	A	Q.16.	D
Q.5.	D	Q.17.	B
Q.6.	B	Q.18.	A
Q.7.	A	Q.19.	C
Q.8.	C	Q.20.	C
Q.9.	C	Q.21.	B
Q.10.	B	Q.22.	D
Q.11.	A	Q.23.	A
Q.12.	D	Q.24.	A

3

Designing a Training Programme

Design must reflect the practical and aesthetics in business but above all...a good design must primarily serve people.

—Thomas J. Watson

After assessing training needs, the training programmes manager will come to know whether training is the right solution to the performance or compliance problem. If training is seen as a solution to the problem, then the training process moves to the next stage i.e. designing a programme. Design is a planning activity which in the context of training, refers to the framework for analyzing a training problem, defining the intended outcome, determining how to present the content to learners to achieve those outcomes, developing the training course according to the design, implementing the course, evaluating its effectiveness and devising follow-up activities. Training design or instructional training is the process of creating a blueprint for the development of instructions.

Whether training is to be conducted in a classroom, delivered using an electronic format or using some combination of methods, the design process sets the stage for the development of a programme that produces results. The effectiveness of a training and development programme depends largely on its design. Designing successful training programmes requires not only a thorough understanding of the training problem, but also a well stated definition of the results to be achieved and a thought out plan for achieving those results. The design of a training programme can be undertaken only when clear training objectives have been produced.

Training designers will have to consider certain important factors from three perspectives before designing a programme and the three perspectives include cost, availability and appropriateness of the training programme. Training designers will have to answer the following questions: What materials will be required to implement the programme in a particular way? What media will be used? And what specialized expertise will be required for implementation of this design?

3.1 Fundamentals of Training Design

It is not an easy task to design a training programme in an organization, as it is dependent on a number of personal factors of the employees involved. Moreover, designing a training programme is a continuous activity. What is happening in most of the organizations is that designing a training programme is given only a lip service and theoretical importance. If an organization wants to get the best out of its employees, it must design training programmes continuously and effectively. However, there are nine fundamentals to designing an effective training programme and each of these elements is discussed in greater detail below.

3.1.1 Mode of Delivery: Mode of delivery in training programme is an important and foremost element of training programme designing. It refers to the method through which training can be imparted to the employees.

3.1.2 Duration of the Programme: The duration of a training programme generally depends upon the nature of the programme. Training duration refers to the length of time that training lasts or continues. Training designer should give careful thought to how much time to allocate for the training course. There is no ideal length of a training session. Optimal length will be based on the complexity of the subject matter to be addressed, skills and prior experience of the participants and information retention capacities of the trainees.

3.1.3 Types of Programmes: Type of the programme should be kept in mind, while designing. There are many types of the training programme, namely:

1. Content updating programmes.
2. Information dissemination programmes.

3. Skill development programmes.
4. Competency enhancement programmes.
5. Attitude development programmes.
6. Rehabilitation programmes.
7. Motivational programmes.
8. Employment generation programmes.
9. Examination/certification programmes.

3.1.4 Target Audience: Audience is one of the most important elements of a training programme. Before designing a training programme, an organization needs to know what their audience is required to learn. A target audience is a group of trainees that the organization has decided to provide a training programme. A well-defined target audience is an important element of a training programme design. Audience can be in the form of:

1. New target employees.
2. Old target employees.
3. Male target audience.
4. Female target audience.
5. Mixed target audience.

3.1.5 Venue of the Programme: Venue of the training plays an important role in designing a training programme. Training venue is a place or location where a training programme will take place. While deciding the venue of the training programme, a training designer should consider following points:

1. Ambience of the training venue.
2. Accessibility of the venue.
3. Ease and comfort.
4. Boarding and lodging.
5. Working conditions.
6. Amenities.
7. Facilities.
8. Transit distance.

3.1.6 Prerequisites of Training: Training helps an organization to achieve the desired organizational goals. Training improves the performance of employees by filling the gap between what is expected from them and what they achieved. A good training programme must possess following characteristics:

1. Exceptional training plan.
2. Training strategies.
3. Resource plan.
4. Mechanism to inform prerequisites to participants.
5. Mechanism to assess participant's expectations.
6. Training delivery plan.
7. Training assessment plan.
8. Contingency plan to meet constraints.

3.1.7 Resource Plan: A resource plan addresses how the training will be resourced and what supporting services, infrastructure and outside trainers will be required to impart training. Resource plans enable organizations to maximize resource utilization, and reduce the gap between desired and actual training requirement. A training resource plan will look at an organization's rather than an individual's training needs.

3.1.8 Training Support Services: Training support services refers to the aids, devices, equipment, and services provided to facilitate efficient operation and maintenance of the training process or system.

3.1.9 Training Plan: A training plan will outline who will deliver the training, and when and where an apprentice or trainee needs to go to receive the structured component of the training. A training plan must be devised within three months of an apprentice or trainee commencing their apprenticeship or traineeship and prior to the delivery of any structured training.

3.1.10 Instructional Event: Instructional event is defined as a systematic process that is employed to develop education and training programmes in a consistent and reliable fashion.

3.1.11 Success Indicators of Training: Training designers are ultimately responsible for delivering a successful training. Organizations should try to find out whether they are able to achieve the training objectives by using the relevant tools and techniques. The main success can be indicated with the help of the following tools:

1. Formal feedback on training.
2. Informal feedback.
3. Retention ratio.
4. Repeat ratio.
5. Voluntary involvement index.

3.2 Why Should an Organization Design a Training Session?

When an organization does decide to design and run a training session, employees will often notice that proper designing of a training programme has several reasons for an organization. A few of them have been discussed below:

1. **To Develop an Individualized Plan Training That Will Best Suit an Organization's Needs:** Proper designing of the training programme can help an organization to achieve the organizational goals in a proper way. An individual development plan is prepared by an employee in partnership with his or her supervisor.
2. **To Pass on the Experience and Expertise of Members of the Organization:** Proper designing of the training programme can help employees to get proper experience and skills from the training programme. Trainers should pass knowledge, ability and skills to the trainees to help them enhance their conceptual and interpersonal skill.
3. **To Give Staff Members Experience in Training Design:** Proper training programme can be a good way to help people improve their confidence in what they know and can do.
4. **To Offer the Staff Additional Opportunities for Professional Growth:** Designing and offering trainings to employees and volunteers is a good way to keep them learning and interested.

3.3 Who Should Design a Training Session?

Organizations need a fair-sized working group to design a training programme.

1. **Experts***:* Experts are widely recognized as a reliable source of techniques or skills. An expert, more generally,

is a person with extensive knowledge or ability based on research, experience, or occupation in a particular area of study. Experienced employees of a particular topic can design a training programme, as they have a prolonged or intense experience through practice and application in a particular field.

2. **Future Learners:** The main purpose of training is to impart knowledge and skill among the employees. These are the people who can help to keep an organization grounded, and let them know if organizational plans regarding designing a training programme are appropriate to increase employee skills and experience. However, it is very important to choose future learners, especially if they are younger or less educated than other members of the training design team, but in this case, an organization should try to choose people who are outgoing and not easily cowed by older or more educated people.
3. **Future Trainers:** Organizations can use future teachers to design a training programme. It will help the organization to ensure that they are comfortable with the material they will be teaching. It is also likely that they will have many other helpful suggestions, especially if they already have experience in formal or informal education.

3.4 Desirable Elements of a Training Programme

1. Training and development programme should be motivating.
2. Attitude, knowledge and skills of the participants.
3. Contents should be divided into modules.
4. There should be activities, recreational programmes and mind games.
5. Training and development should be participative.
6. Training and development programme should cover all the relevant contents.
7. Combination of training and development should be used.
8. It should focus on proper group sizes.
9. It should start from simple to complex contents.

10. It should focus on the available resources.

3.5 Steps Involved in Designing a Training and Development Programme

Developing an effective employee training programme is vital to the long-term success of any organization. Training programmes can provide multiple benefits for employees and the company, but only if training programmes are cautiously designed and properly implemented. Proper designing of training and development can lead to increased motivation, morale and productivity for employees, and higher profits for an organization. Hence, designing an effective training programme is built by following a planned, systematic and organized step-by-step procedure. In today's world, following necessary steps to designing an effective programme should be kept in mind:

3.5.1 Define Clearly Objectives of Training and Development: It is a very pertinent step for designing a training and development programme in an organization. Training objective refers to the specific results that an organization aims to achieve within a time frame and with available resources. Generally, objectives are more specific and easier to measure than goals. These are the basic tools that underlie all planning and strategic activities. They serve as the basis for creating policy and evaluating performance of the participants. Hence, the main purpose of an objective in training is a clear statement of the performance to be achieved and should define what participants will be expected to learn or do as a result of participating in training programme.

3.5.2 Selecting Trainers: Once the organization has made decision to design its own training programme, next step is to select a trainer. Selecting a trainer is probably the most important decision in an organization, as his or her judgment and expertise will be invaluable both now and in the future. Therefore, trainer should be selected scientifically, trained appropriately, motivated enough with proper service conditions and provided with development opportunities and feedback to improve their capabilities continuously. Successful trainers involve the trainee's right from the beginning to evolve the lesson plan, identify learning methodology, and benchmark best practices. Trainers teach in the ways appropriate for the trainees rather than those appropriate for themselves.

3.5.3 Who can be a Trainer? There are many people who may be selected to develop, facilitate, and evaluate a training programme. Training activities can be provided by several people, listed below:

1. **Supervisors and Managers:** These days, on the job training is the only method of training offered to the employees in an organization. In this situation, supervisors and managers are the providers of whatever training employees receive. Supervisors and managers are appropriate in assisting in development activities that involve mentoring, as they are in the best position to assess their employee's career needs.
2. **Co-workers:** Co-workers are more well-informed about the work than anyone else. They play an important role in management development progamme, which commonly brings together employees from different divisions of an organization for several days of training. Participants in such programmes often report that the most valuable training occurs through conversations with their colleagues.
3. **Experts:** It is generally seen that subject matter experts may not be familiar with procedures in a specific organizational culture. As a result, they may be respected for their expertise, but mistrusted because they are not members of the working community. However, organizations should choose an expert who is expressive and well organized while delivering a training.
4. **Employee:** Self-paced instruction is also an option. With the growing popularity of computer-based training, self-paced instruction is also becoming more frequent. Trainees benefit from this method in learning at a speed that maximizes retention.

3.6 Designing Training and Development Module

After selecting the trainer, next step is to design the training and development module. Training and development module are the heart and soul of a structured training programme. Designing training modules involve creating a package of material about a specific subject or activity from which people can learn. It is important to be clear for whom the module is meant for. Whether it is for a subject or activity, both types of training modules are similar in nature as they contain clearly stated learning objectives and a sound structure with user-friendly supporting materials. The content for training modules should be developed by a team of employees who do the job on a regular basis. Having teams create the module speeds up the process dramatically.

Ideally, the team should consist of employees who are subject matter experts, those workers who are knowledgeable in the job but not experts yet, as well as trainees or newcomers who do not know the job can also be included. With this diverse group, an organization will be sure to develop the training at just the right level for trainees. When subject matter experts alone develop the training material, it may be "*over the heads*" of most trainees or may leave out important information that the trainee might not feel comfortable questioning in a training situation.

3.7 Selecting Training and Development Methods

After deciding the training and development module, the next step is to select the training and development method, through which the training is to be imparted. Training and development method is defined as a systematic procedure used by the trainer for the development of skills of employees in an organization. There is a huge array and variety of training methods each with its advantages and disadvantages. The use of a particular method depends which method accomplishes the training needs and objectives. Combination of these methods contributes to the effectiveness of a training and development programme. By altering the training method the trainer uses, he can keep learners interested, activate different learning styles and enhance compensation and retention.

3.8 Training and Development Materials

Once the trainer has decided on the method or methods to be used for the training programme, the next step in designing is preparing the training material. This becomes more important for programme designed in-house than for training programmes provided from outside. Training and development materials are resources if used properly, could assist trainers in achieving the specific training objectives and carrying out the training assignment in a more effective manner. Training and development material refers to the resource and support facilities used by instructors, facilitators, and students in a training environment. These materials store the information needed by the learners to perform tasks. Training material can be classified into two categories: printed or recorded information used in a training programme. Training equipment required for training and development programme may vary from the usual classroom requirements like white boards, markers, flip charts etc. to electronic equipments and gadgets.

3.9 General Guidelines for Planning the Content of the Course Material

1. Be specific and address the needs of the trainees.
2. Each topic should only be given a sufficient amount of time it will take to cover the most important points.
3. Course material should have flexibility, so that trainees are able to spend more time on some topics if the need arises.
4. Be prepared for unexpected questions and problems. When answering questions, always be honest in your response. If you do not know the answer, think of other resources to recommend on the subject in question.
5. Prepare general time guidelines for each session, but remember the need for flexibility. It can be helpful to put together a plan for the training, which should be displayed in a visible location in the room during the whole training

session. The visibility of the training plan will positively influence the learning process, as it allows the participants to clearly see the objectives of the training session.

6. Trainer should prepare concise, usable written materials. Course outlines do not need to be long.
7. Use visual support system throughout.
8. Trainer must focus on the participation of the employees. He should involve the participants as early as possible in the programme. They should remember that it can be difficult to sit and listen to a presentation for more than one hour.
9. A trainer should consider team approach while planning course structure.

3.10 Training and Development Schedule

A training schedule or a timetable is a basic time management tool consisting of a list of times at which possible tasks, events, or actions are intended to take place or a sequence of events in the chronological order in which such things are intended to take place. The process of creating a training schedule deciding how to perform these tasks and how to use available resources between the variety of possible tasks is called training scheduling, and the person responsible for making a particular trainer schedule may be called a training scheduler. It provides a detail of who, what, when and how specific events are to be addressed during the planning of a training programme. This also prevents misunderstandings, and any schedule conflicts can be worked out early.

3.11 Spiral Model of Training

In this method, training inputs are provided both by the work organizations and training organizations. Organizations have built-in training system and also engage outside institutions for training. Due to built-in system, training has a starting and continues as a process with three continuous phases of pre-training, training, and post-training and hence it is called a spiral model. The sub-phases of each phase along with work organizations and training institution's inputs is described below. The Spiral Model of training centres on training risks. More specifically, it is concerned with how to minimize training risks so that an organization can achieve the desired results. An organization and trainer is involved in every step of the way to improve the design of the training and remedy unforeseen issues. Barry Boehm first introduced the Spiral Model back in 1988. Steps involved in a Spiral Model are as follows:

1. Identify training needs and break down the training budget.
2. Set a realistic design and development schedule.
3. Create communication guidelines.
4. Determine the risks involved and create alternative training methods.
5. Develop a phased model.
6. Gather trainee's feedback at each stage.
7. Reassess training risks periodically.
8. Use trainee's input to continually improve the training programme.

3.11.1 Advantages of the Spiral SDLC Model:

1. Changing requirements of training can be accommodated.
2. Allows extensive use of training methods.
3. Training requirements can be captured more accurately.
4. Training can be imparted into smaller parts and the risky parts can be developed earlier which helps in better training risk management.

3.11.2 Disadvantages of the Spiral SDLC Model:

1. Training management is more complex.
2. Outcome of the training may not be known early.
3. Process is complex.
4. Spiral may go on indefinitely.
5. Large number of training intermediate stages requires excessive documentation.

At the end we can say that, deigning of a training programme plays an important role in the training process. More importantly, an effective training programme is built by following an organized and systematic process. Ineffective and unorganized training programme that stand alone, may often fail to meet the organizational objectives, training objectives, trainer's purpose and participant's expectations.

3.12 Summary

1. Design is a planning activity which in the context of training, refers to the framework for analyzing a training problem, defining the intended outcome, determining how to present the content to learners to achieve those outcomes, developing the training course according to the design, implementing the course, evaluating its effectiveness and devising follow-up activities.
2. Training design or instructional training is the process of creating a blueprint for the development of instructions.
3. There are nine fundamentals to design an effective training programme. They include:
   - Mode of delivery.
   - Duration of the programme.
   - Type of programme.
   - Target audience.
   - Venue of the programme.
   - Prerequisites of training.
   - Resource requirement.
   - Training support system.
   - Success indicators.
4. Experts, future learners and teachers should design a training programme.
5. The training and development design consists of following steps: defining clear objectives of training and development, selecting trainers, designing training development module, selecting training and development methods, and developing a training and development schedule.
6. Training and development material refers to the resource and support facilities used by instructors, facilitators, and students in a training environment.
7. Transitional model describes a double loop of corporate

strategy and learning.

Short Answer Type Questions

1. While selecting a training venue what points a training manager should keep in mind?
2. Who are target audience?
3. What is a resource plan?
4. Define training plan.
5. Who can be a trainer?
6. How training module can be prepared?
7. Define training schedule.

Long Answer Type Questions

1. Explain the meaning and significance of a training design.
2. Enumerate important considerations to be kept in mind while designing a training and development programme.
3. Discuss various factors to be taken into account for designing a training programme.
4. Discuss the steps of spiral model of training.
5. Describe the characteristics of an effective training design.
6. Discuss the fundamentals of training design.
7. Why should an organisation design a training session? Comment.
8. Discuss the various steps for developing a training material.
9. What is training material and how it is developed?
10. What are the various guidelines for planning the content of a course material?
11. Who should design a training session?

Multiple Choice Questions

Q. 1. Which of the following is a benefit of employee training?

a. Improves morale
b. Helps people identify organizational goals
c. Provides good climate for learning and growth
d. None of the above

Q. 2. Choose which of the following is a benefit to an individual while receiving the training?

a. Creates an appropriate climate for growth
b. Aids in increasing productivity
c. Satisfies personal needs of the trainer
d. None of the above

Q. 3. Which of these is a step in training process?

a. KSA deficiency
b. Providing proper feedback
c. Obstacles in the system
d. Use of evaluation models

Q. 4. Which of the following is a method used in group or organizational needs assessment?

a. Consideration of current and projected changes
b. Rating scales
c. Interviews
d. Questionnaires

Q. 5. _______ seeks to examine the goals of the organization and the trends that are likely to affect these goals

a. Organizational support
b. Organizational analysis
c. Person analysis
d. Key skill abilities analysis

Q. 6. Which of these is a benefit of needs assessment?

a. Assessment makes training department more accountable
b. Higher training costs
c. Loss of business
d. Increased overtime working

Q. 7. Which of the following is a learning principle?

a. Recognition of individual differences
b. Schedules of learning
c. Transfer of learning
d. All of the above

Q. 8. Which of these is a hindrance to effective training?
a. Career planning workshop
b. Aggregate spending on training being inadequate
c. Mentoring
d. Counselling

Q. 9. In an organization, the technique which plays a significant role in person-organization fit after employee selection is classified as
a. Job enhancement
b. Job orientation
c. Job enrichment
d. Job enlargement

Q. 10. The concept in training of employees in which the reason of training must be told to trainees about why it is necessary is called
a. Whole learning
b. Tactile learning
c. Gestalt learning
d. Both a and c

Q. 11. The systematic introduction to employees about their new job, the co-workers on workplace and about the organization is classified as
a. Job enhancement
b. Job orientation
c. Job enrichment
d. Job enlargement

Q. 12. The concept which states that the trainee must have the belief to learn the content of the training program is classified as
a. Intervening efficacy
b. Auditory efficacy
c. Learner readiness
d. Self-efficacy

Q. 13. Which of the following helps to create a more relaxed atmosphere for the participants?
a. Humour
b. Voice
c. Tone
d. Vocabulary

Q. 14. What are the possible benefits to train an employee using new technology?
(1) Reading and writing skills are improved
(2) Improves employee morale
(3) Self-confidence and skill levels are improved
a. Only (1) and (2)
b. All of these
c. Only (2) and (3)
d. Only (1) and (3)

Q. 15. What was the need for developing the concept of learning style?
a. To not classify learners
b. To classify learners
c. None of these
d. To help organizations

Q. 16. _______ is not considered as a part of competency design framework
a. People competency
b. Logistical competency
c. Technical competency
d. Administrative competency

Q. 17. The first step of training management cycle is
a. Planning
b. Evaluation
c. Implementation
d. None of these

Q. 18. What all is included when trainees take responsibility for learning and transfer?

a. Preparing for training
b. Being involved and engaged during training
c. Using training content back on the job
d. All of the above

Q. 19. What problem is a trainee likely to encounter in the work environment that inhibit transfer of training?

a. Factors related to the work itself
b. Lack of support from peers and managers
c. Both option a and b
d. None of the above

Q. 20. Which among the following act as a parameter to determine the intelligence/potential for learning of an individual?

a. Academic discipline
b. Human capital
c. Intelligent quotient
d. Learning styles

Answer Key

Q.1.	B	Q.11.	B
Q.2.	C	Q.12.	D
Q.3.	D	Q.13.	A
Q.4.	A	Q.14.	C
Q.5.	B	Q.15.	B
Q.6.	A	Q.16.	B
Q.7.	D	Q.17.	B
Q.8.	B	Q.18.	C
Q.9.	B	Q.19.	C
Q.10.	D	Q.20.	C

4

Training Methods and Techniques

For years, organizations around the world would need to take decisions regarding the structure of training in an organization. Training structure describes a training framework. It establishes a pattern of relationship among the constituent parts of the training. Large organizations with HR departments typically have training and development experts on roll. In a HR department led by a vice president or a director, there might be a training and development manager also as well as training specialists.

4.1 Types of Training

Training and development managers collaborate with senior HR executives to determine the role that training plays in the strategic direction of HR and the overall organization. They are experts in adult learning theory, methods and application and they might be equally well-versed in organizational development. Training specialists are the ones who conduct classroom training, web-based instructions and in-house workshops.

There are two types of structural training listed below:

1. **Centralized Training:** Centralized training is the process by which the decision-making authority regarding training within an organization becomes centralized in a particular location or a group, usually at the top management level and decision about training, investment, programmes, and delivery are made from that department.
2. **Decentralized Training:** These days, organizations are continuously rearranging and streamlining their training programmes to survive in an immense competitive world occurring from global expansion, the assault of new technologies and other factors beyond their control. Decentralization is one in which a training function is

operated independently by certain entities throughout an enterprise.

4.2 On the Job Training

On the job training (OJT) methods are commonly used in training for all levels of employees. Every employee from lower to top level gets 'on the job training', when he joins an organization. The main purpose of on the job training is to bring the employees to at least a minimum acceptable standard of performance in the minimum time. It is a traditional method of learning, where workers learn to master the operations involved in the actual job situation under the supervision of his immediate boss, instructor, and trainer. It is preferable for unskilled and semi-skilled jobs and clerical and sales jobs also. In most organizations, on the job training for new employees is followed by an induction programme where new employees are made aware of an organization's culture, policies, practices and procedures and for interaction of new employees with others. On the job training is also known as *shop training*.

4.2.1 Advantages: On the job training offers several benefits to the organization and those are as under:

1. **Simple:** On the job training is a simple method of training. In this method, the trainer need not explain and analyze the job details, as a trainee can learn it by doing on his/her own.
2. **Economical:** OJT is economical as it does not require additional resources for arranging training needs and it does not need separate training space.
3. **Learning:** OJT offers a constructive atmosphere for learning.
4. **Actual Work environment:** OJT is conducted in the actual work environment; hence, employees can get a firsthand experience from the job as they learn it through actual equipments and materials.
5. **Immediate Results:** Since trainees are involved in an actual work process, quick learning and immediate results will be obtained from the work performed by the trainees.
6. **Multi-skill:** It develops multi-skill tasking in trainees. The

employees can get quick feedback about correctness of their performance from their boss, instructor and trainer.

4.2.2 Job Rotation: Job rotation is a management approach where employees are shifted from one job to another at regular intervals of time. It is a pre-planned approach where one re eives job knowledge and gains experience from his supervisor or trainer in each of the different job assignments. Moreover, it reduces the boredom of the job and gives them a wider experience and helps them gain more insights. One accomplishes a better sense of his/her own career objectives and interest. This method gives an opportunity to the trainee to understand the problems of employees in other jobs. This method permits the trainees to build empathy with large number of employees within the organization and facilitate cooperation among individuals. Job rotation can improve employees' understanding of the business strategy, functions, and divisions of the company as well as help them develop valuable contacts.

Job rotation offers several benefits to an organization. It reduces monotony of the job; develops a pool of employees; helps create a right employee for the right job; exposes employees to all verticals of the company; tests employee skills and competencies; and develops a wider range of work experience.

There are two types of job rotation:

1. **Task Rotation:** It is concerned with the jobs that involve a high degree of physical demands on the body, since high degree of repetitive tasks can become extremely monotonous. These days, employees are facing stress and frustration for their monotonous job nature. To remove their stress and frustration, employees are periodically shifted from these mentally stressful or physically demanding tasks to a less demanding task for a while to give them a break.
2. **Position Rotation:** It is concerned with moving an employee to different positions, departments or geographical locations for the purpose of professionally developing an employee by exposing them to new knowledge, skills and perspectives. It can be further broken down into *within-function rotation* and

cross-functional rotation. Within-function rotation is where an employee rotates between jobs with similar levels of responsibility and in the same functional or operational areas. Cross-functional rotation, on the other hand, refers to a sequence of positions, often with increasing levels of job responsibilities.

Job rotation provides advantages for an employee in following ways:

1. It helps in gaining knowledge and skills by learning different jobs.
2. It helps in overcoming potential boredom and job dissatisfaction by having a new and different job with changed responsibilities and tasks.
3. It helps in presenting new challenges and opportunities for an employee to expand his or her knowledge.
4. It helps employees to learn about different facets of the organization and how work is accomplished in different departments.
5. It prepares an employee for an eventual promotion.
6. It helps employees to gain visibility with a new group of co-workers and supervisors.

4.2.3 Coaching: Coaching is an important and most commonly used tool in the job training method. Coaching is a kind of daily training and feedback given to the employees by immediate supervisors. Coaching is a training process where trainer is supported while performing the job or task in an organization. It may be defined as an informal, unplanned training provided by the supervisor and peers. It involves direct instruction and supervision, usually with demonstration and continuous appraisal and correction. Coaching with highly capable colleagues helps employees progress and gives them the opportunity to share ideas and goals with each other. In this regard, the supervisor provides feedback to the trainee on a continuous basis and offers him some suggestions for improvement. Trainee shares some of the duties and responsibilities of the coach and relieves him of his burden. It is one of the training methods, which is considered as a corrective method for inadequate performance.

Following are the characteristics of coaching:

1. Managers train all of their employees as a required part of the job.
2. Coaching takes place within the borders of a formal employer-employee relationship.
3. Focuses on developing employees within their current jobs.
4. Interest is functional, arising out of the need to ensure that individuals can perform the tasks required to the best of their abilities.
5. Relationship tends to be initiated and driven by an individual's manager.
6. Relationship is finite—ends as an individual transfers to another job.

4.2.4 Apprenticeship Training: Apprenticeship training is the oldest and most commonly used method of training in industrial craft, trades and technical areas. Many organizations use this method to impart training to their employees. Craft workers such as plumbers and carpenters are trained through formal apprenticeship programme. It helps prepare and train employees for a career in a skilled trade or craft. It combines supervised on the job training with job related classroom instructions to teach trainees the practical and theoretical aspects of a highly skilled occupation. Assistantship and internship are similar to apprenticeship because both approaches demand high level of involvement from the employees. Apprenticeship like coaching, attempts to provide a model to copy for trainees. In India, the government has established industrial training institutes (ITIs) for this purpose, where theoretical instructions and practical learning is provided to the trainees.

The main purpose of apprenticeship training is to develop all around craftsmen or skilled workforce. Apprentices are paid while gaining work experience, and their wages increase with their levels of skill. From an organizational prospective, apprenticeship programmes meet specific business training needs and help attract talented employees. The duration of training depends upon the intensity of training. But there are some cases where the period of training is specified even from 5 to 7 years. In most cases, the apprenticeship period extends to 4 years including curriculum of classroom and shop experience. Each apprentice is given a programme of assignments according to a pre-determined schedule, which provides training in trade skills.

The merits of this method are as under:

1. A skilled workforce is sustained.
2. The workmanship is good.
3. Direct return can be expected from training.
4. The loyalty of an employee increases and opportunities for growth are prevalent.
5. The recruitment and selection costs are lower as is reduced employee turnover and absenteeism.

4.2.5 Job Instruction Training (JIT): The JIT method (developed during World War II), is a structural method where a trainer prepares a trainee to perform better at a workplace with the help of four steps involving: preparation, presentation, performance and follow up. This method is very popular in the United States for preparing supervisors to train operatives. The JIT method involves skilled trainers, broad job analysis, training schedule, and prior assessment of the trainee's job knowledge and skill. In this, a trainer can act as a coach. The main purpose of the JIT is to teach the employees how to do a current job in proper sequence. The coach tells what is to be done. Besides, each step is also listed as a consistent "key point", which shows how it is to be done and why. This method is also known as "training through step-by-step learning". The four steps involved in JIT are given below:

1. **Preparation:** Preparation of a trainee is very important. It involves making trainee comfortable with the environment; explain the job to a trainee; and acclimatize him with the learning process.
2. **Presentation:** It involves giving essential information in a clear manner. It involves telling, showing and illustrating

each and every step; dictating each key point in detail to the trainees and stressing why and how each step should be carried out as it is shown.

3. **Performance Try Out:** In this step, trainer must give time to trainee to perform a task and act like a coach and correct errors if they occur; must explain each key point to trainee during the process; make sure the trainee understands his/her job clearly and must continue the process until the trainee fully understands.
4. **Follow-up:** In this, a trainer must let the trainee work independently; assign a person to go to for assistance; check frequently and encourage questions and follow up regularly.

4.3 Syndicate Method

A syndicate is primarily a study group, the members of which represent the principal sub-groups participating in the programme. The syndicate has a chairperson and a secretary, the positions of which are generally held in rotation by the participants. A problem is assigned to the syndicate for study and solution. The group works on its own, with only minimum guidance from the training staff, makes its own library studies, collects data, exchanges views and experience, avails itself of the facility of consulting specialists in the field, and finally prepares a report on the assignment. The report of each syndicate is presented to an assembly of the training faculty and all the syndicates in the training programme as a whole for comments and discussion. The study on any subject may continue for a month or more, with 10 to 12 sittings.

4.4 Knowledge-based Methods

In this method, an attempt is made to impart an employee, knowledge in any subject area covering aspects like its concepts and theories, basic principles and pure and applied knowing of the subject. The common methods that fall into this category are described hereunder:

4.4.1 Classroom Lectures: This method is a traditional and direct method of instructions. Lecture method is well-known method to train managerial level employees in an organization. Lecture is a verbal presentation of information by an instructor to a large number of employees. Lectures are formal organized talks by training specialists on individual specific topics. To be effective, the lecture must motivate and create interest among the employees. This method is used for the purpose of teaching administrative aspects. The main purpose of classroom lecture is to create an understanding of a topic and to influence behaviour and attitude through lecture. A lecture can be in the form of written or oral. It generally helps to enhance the skills of listeners and to apprise them of the theoretical aspects of a topic. Advantages and disadvantages of lecture method are outlined in Table 4.1.

4.4.2 Programmed Training: Programmed training has become popular in recent years. Under this method, the subject matter to be learnt is in the form of carefully planned sequential units which are often set up through the central panel of an electronic computer as a guide in the performance of a preferred process or series of processes.

It includes a pre-arranged, proposed or desired course of measures relating to the learning or achievement of some specific skills or general knowledge. It involves breaking information into meaningful units and then arranging them in a proper fashion to establish a logical and sequential learning programme.

It can also be a computer-enabled one, with the use of computer terminals, video discs, light pen, touch screen, main frame, mini and micro computers. In such a programme, knowledge is imparted with the use of a textbook or a teaching machine.

The programme involves presenting questions and facts or problems to the trainee to utilize the information given, and subsequently, a trainee instantly receives feedback in the form of correct answers. This method is primarily used in teaching factual knowledge, such as mathematics, physics, a foreign language, etc.

The main purpose of this method is to give sufficient

information to the learners and then test their command over the subject matter.

Table 4.1: Advantages and Disadvantages of Lecture Method

Advantages	Disadvantages
It can be used for large group of trainees	The attention span of even a well-motivated and adequately informed listener is from 15 minutes to 20 minutes only; in the course of an hour, the interest of an employee drifts
Time and cost per trainee is low	Lecture method violates the principle of learning by doing
Classroom lectures allow the instructor to have maximum control of the learning experience	It is one-way communication. The learners are passive instead of active participants
Lectures appeal to those who learn by listening	There is no authentic feedback mechanism
	A clear and vigorous verbal presentation requires a great deal of preparation for which management personnel often lack time
Lectures can be specifically organized to meet the needs of particular audiences	Lectures presume that all students learn at the same pace and are at the same level of understanding
	Students' attention wanes quickly after fifteen to twenty-five minutes

The essence of this method is that it emphasizes frequent questions, small steps, immediate and accurate feedback. Advantages and disadvantages of programmed training are given in Table 4.2.

4.4.3 Conference: This is also an old method, but still a favourite training method. In order to escape the limitations of straight lecturing, many organizations have adopted guided-discussion types of conferences in their training programmes. Conference refers to the holding of a group meeting conducted according to an organized and systematic plan in which the members seek to develop knowledge and understanding by getting a considerable participation. This method is beneficial in the case of imparting training for persons in the positions of both conference members and conference leaders.

Table 4.2: Advantages and Disadvantages of Programmed Training

Advantages	Disadvantages
It needs less time	The scope of programmed learning is quite less as only factual subject matters can be programmed
Trainees learn at their own pace	Philosophical and attitudinal concept and motor skills cannot be taught
It helps trainees to learn the subject matter at their own speed	It requires more resources for preparing books, manuals and machinery
Instructors are not a key part in learning	The cost of programmed training is quite high
Strong motivation is provided to the trainees	
Material used in this training is also structured	
Immediate feedback is available	
Training can take place at odd times and in odd places	

In this method, an individual can learn from others by comparing his opinions, feelings and conclusions with those of others. It helps to develop an employee's skills by motivating them through the direction of discussion. In conference method, all the participants learn from each other. Therefore, it is preferably suitable to sort out learning problems and issues and examine them from several angles. As such, it can also serve as an ideal method for reducing the dogmatism that is employed in supervisory and training programmes.

4.5 Simulation Methods

Simulation method of training is quite famous and a foundational method of training. Simulation involves creating an environment which is similar to real life situations. Simulation technique is widely used in the aeronautical industry. Trainees' interest and employee motivation are high in simulation exercise because the actions of trainees closely duplicate real job conditions.

The simulation method essentially engages the acting out or performance by participants or trainees simulated business behaviour in reaching decisions and implementing them. This method helps a trainee to handle stress, take decisions, and handling pressure on the jobs. The main propose of simulation is to teach production skills, process skills, and interpersonal skills in an exciting and memorable way.

Advantages and disadvantages of simulation are given in Table 4.3.

Table 4.3: Advantages and Disadvantages of Simulation

Advantages	Disadvantages
Simulation creates interest and motivation among the employees	It involves huge cost
This type of training is very useful to avoid any costly errors	This method needs constant up-gradation
Trainee can concentrate on learning without involving much risk	In simulation, role playing is done in an artificial environment which is impractical
It provides feedback to the trainer and trainee to modify their behaviour	It does not emphasize on teaching skills or content taught. It focuses only on social behaviour of the individuals
It helps in developing social skills and etiquettes among the trainers and trainees	Simulation training is very complex and difficult as it is very difficult to portray the real situation
There is a self-monitoring in simulated training	

4.5.1 Case Study: Case study is a written description of an actual situation in the past. This is based upon the belief that managerial competencies can best be attained through study, contemplation, and discussion of concrete cases. In this, trainee is given with some written material and some complex situations of a real or imaginary organization. This method involves studying cases from all perspectives, analyzing various alternatives available to the company for solving problems or address issues and arriving at the most suitable answers in writing. Case is later discussed by instructor with all the pros and cons of each option. Trainers develop a habit of looking at problems from various perspectives and hence their decisions as managers will be more realistic and based on sound study and analysis. This is an excellent method to ensure full involvement and participation of the employees. It is an ideal method to promote decision-making abilities within the constraints of limited data (Table 4.4).

Table 4.4: Advantages and Disadvantages of Case Study

Advantages	Disadvantages
It promotes analytical thinking and develops a person's problem solving ability among the participants	It may lead to restrain in voice of average trainees as only those having more analytical and vocal skills will dominate the sessions
It involves action, doing and practice	Results are not quite certain
It encourages open mindedness, participation and involvement among the participants. It serves as a means of integrating the knowledge obtained from different basic disciplines	It involves more resources in the form of energy, time and finance
It is acceptable to everyone as it deals with detailed description of real life situations	

4.5.2 Vestibule Training: Vestibule training utilizes the equipment which closely resembles the actual ones used in a job.

This training is given to employees when new or advanced equipment, machinery or tool is introduced in an organization. Most of the times, this method of training is given to train technical staff, office staff and employees who deal with tools and machines. A special room is set aside from the main production area and is equipped with furnishings similar to the actual production area. Afterwards, the trainees are given an opportunity to learn under simulated conditions. This method involves taking trainees through a short planned course of instructions and practices, in offices and shops, in a simulated real working environment. Such training usually takes from a few days to a few weeks. This method is used where a few skills and knowledge are required to be learnt (Table 4.5).

Table 4.5: Advantages and Disadvantages of Vestibule Training

Advantages	Disadvantages
This training is helpful to train large number of employees in a short span of time	It is an expensive method because of the additional investment in classrooms, equipment and expert trainers
It allows trainees to practice without the fear of being observed	Vestibule training does not provide the feeling of an actual environment
This method is free from any pressure of getting out on production	This method is limited for few jobs
It helps to increase the motivation level of employees	
This method focuses on learning without disturbance of the workplace noise	

4.5.3 In-basket Method: In-basket method is a method where a trainee is required to examine a basket full of papers and files relating to his area of work and make recommendations on problems contained therein. This method is meant for learners at a managerial level to improve their decision-making and policy-making ability, and use establishment of priorities, delegation, coordination and problem-solving abilities. This is a form of simulation development designed around day-to-day business situations and hence is transferable to the job experiences.

The participant is usually asked to establish priorities and then handle a number of office papers, such as memoranda, reports, telephone messages and emails that would typically cross a manager's desk. The method has at least two main stages. At the outset, the participant starts by working through the case within a specified time limit all by himself without discussing the details with anyone. Subsequently, other participants analyze and discuss the questions of who's, which's, how's, what's, where's, why's and when's of each decision or step.

In this method, a trainee is given some information about the role to be played involving description, responsibilities, and general context about the role. The trainee is then given the log of materials that make up the in-basket and asked to respond to materials within a particular time period. After all the learners complete in-basket, a discussion with the trainer takes place. In this discussion, a trainee describes the explanation for the decisions. The trainer then provides feedback, reinforcing decisions made suitably or encouraging the trainee to increase alternatives for those made unsuitably. A variation on the technique is to run multiple and simultaneous in-baskets in which each trainee receives a different but organized set of information. It is important that learners must communicate with each other to accumulate the entire information required to make a suitable decision.

This method involves two essential elements: (a) a step-by-step series of bits of knowledge, each building upon what has gone before, and (b) a mechanism for presenting the series and checking on the trainee's knowledge.

4.5.4 Laboratory Training: Laboratory training is conducted for groups by skilled trainers. It is generally conducted at a neutral site and is used by upper and middle management trainees to develop a spirit of teamwork and an increased ability to deal with the peers. This training adds to conventional training by providing situations in which trainees themselves experience through their own interaction some of the conditions they are talking about. This way, they more or less experiment on themselves. Laboratory training is more concerned about changing an individual behaviour and attitude. It is generally more successful in transforming job performance than conventional training methods.

4.6 Experiential Methods of Training

4.6.1 Sensitivity Training: Sensitivity training is an experimental approach to training. It is concerned with making people understand about their behaviour and of others. It provides the participants an opportunity to actually experience concepts of management like a manager would face them in his/her own organizational situation. This method is also known as laboratory training. It influences participants through unstructured group interaction. Sensitivity training involves small number of participants usually fewer than 12 in a group. The meetings do not have any agenda, are held away from workplace, and questions deal with the 'here and now' of the group process. The main purposes of sensitivity training are to provide managers with increased awareness of their own behaviour and how others perceive them, greater sensitivity to the behaviours of others, and increased understanding of the group processes.

The main advantage of sensitivity training is that participants remain involved and enthusiastic. Many organizations, irrespective of the industry, have been sending their employees to sensitivity training programmes for years in order to further strengthen the behavioural competencies or understand the applicability of their learning in organizations or of the participants, irrespective of their role in the present job.

4.6.2 Computer-based Training (CBT): Computer-based training is becoming increasingly prevalent as technology becomes more widespread and easy to use. Though traditional forms of training are not likely to be replaced completely by technological solutions, they will most likely be enhanced by them. Human interaction will always remain a key component of workplace training. Nonetheless, it is a good idea to look more closely at what training technologies have to offer and how they might be used to supplement the existing training programs or used when developing new ones. Computer-based training formats vary from the simplest text-only programs to highly sophisticated multimedia programs to virtual reality. Consider the following types:

1. **Text-only:** The simplest computer-based training programs offer self-paced training in a text-only format. These programs are similar to print-based, individualized training modules with the addition, in most cases, of interactive features. While simple in format, these programs can be highly effective and present complicated information and concepts in a comprehensible and easily accessible way.
2. **CD-ROM:** A wide variety of off-the-shelf training programs covering a broad range of workplace topics are available on CD-ROM. Programs can also be created by training consultants for the specific needs of a particular organization or individual departments.
3. **Multimedia:** These training materials are an advanced form of computer-based training. They are much more sophisticated than the original text-only programs. In addition to text, they provide stimulating graphics, audio, animation, and/or video. Multimedia tends to be more proactive and challenging and, therefore, more stimulating to the adult mind. Although costs are higher than text-only software, the benefits in terms of employee learning may well be worth it. Multimedia training materials are typically found in DVD format.
4. **Virtual Reality:** Virtual reality is three-dimensional and interactive, immersing the trainee in a learning experience. Most virtual reality training programs take the form of simulation, which is a highly effective form of training. It is a hands-on experience without the risks of actual performance. Flight simulators, for example, have been used successfully

for years to train airline and military pilots in critical flying skills, as well as to prepare them for emergency situations in a safe and forgiving environment.

Following are the advantages of computer-based training:

1. Computer-based training programs are easy to use.
2. They can often be customized or custom designed.
3. They are good in helping employees develop and practice new skills.
4. They are useful for refresher training.
5. They are applicable to self-directed learning.
6. They can be cost-effective because the same equipment and program can be used by a large numbers of employees.
7. They are flexible because trainees can learn at their own pace and at a time that is convenient for them. Computer-based programs are available 24x7. No matter which shift an employee works, training is always available.
8. Some programs are interactive, requiring trainees to answer questions, make choices, and experience the consequences of those choices. This interaction generally results in greater comprehension and retention.
9. They are uniform, which makes it possible to standardize training.
10. They are measurable. When computers are used for training, it is possible to track what each employee has learnt right on the computer. Most programs have post-tests to determine whether an employee has understood the training. Test scores give trainers statistics for training evaluation.

Following are the disadvantages of computer-based training:

1. These programs require trainees to be computer literate.
2. They require trainees to have computer access.
3. There is little or no interaction with a trainer; if trainees have questions, there is no one to ask.
4. These programs are not effective at teaching "soft-skills", such as customer service, sales, or sensitivity training.
5. They are not the best choice for new or one-time training. Trainers need live interaction to ensure new skills or concepts

are being communicated. Trainees need to be able to ask questions and receive feedback.

6. Some poorly designed programs are "boring" and result in trainees having a poor retention rate of the material as well as a low finish rate.

4.6.3 E-Training: In addition to on the job training methods, many companies with employees in a variety of locations across the country are relying on other technologies to deliver training. This method is becoming more and more popular as access to web becomes widely available. Some examples include:

1. **Web-based Training.** This method puts computer-based training modules onto the web, which companies can then make available to their employees either on the company's intranet or on a section of the vendor's website that is set up for the company. There are many courses available on the internet in many different topic areas. These courses provide a hands-on, interactive way for employees to work through training presentations that are similar to CD-ROM or PowerPoint.
2. **Tele- or Video Conferencing:** These methods allow the trainer to be in one location and trainees to be scattered in several locations. Participants are networked into the central location and can usually ask questions to the trainer via telephone or by a webchat feature. Lectures and demonstrations can be effective using this method.
3. **Audio Conferencing:** This method is similar to video conferencing but involves audio only. Participants dial in at the scheduled meeting time and hear speakers present their training. Question and answer sessions are frequently held at the end of sessions in which participants can email questions or call in and talk to the presenter.
4. **Web Meetings or Webinars:** This method contains audio and visual components. Participants dial in to receive live audio training and also follow visual material that appears on their computer screens.
5. **Online Colleges and Universities:** This method is also

known as distance learning, and many universities now offer certificates or degrees through online programs that require only minimal on-campus residency.

6. **Collaborative Document Preparation:** This method requires participants to be linked on the same network. It can be used with coaches and trainees to teach writing reports and technical documents.
7. **Email:** You can use email to promote or enhance training or send reminders for upcoming training. One can also solicit follow-up questions for trainers and/or managers and conduct training evaluations through e-mail forms.

Following are the advantages of e-training:

1. Online or e-learning programs are effective for training across multiple locations.
2. They save the company, money on travel expenses.
3. They can be a less expensive way to get training from expert industry professionals and consultants from outside the company.
4. They are useful for refresher training.
5. They are good for self-directed learning.
6. They can be easy to update with new company policies or procedures, government regulations, and compliance issues.
7. They offer trainers a growing array of choices for matching training programs to employee knowledge and skill levels.

Following are the disadvantages of e-training:

1. These programs require trainees to be computer literate.
2. They are usually generic and not customized to a company's needs.
3. Some employees may not like the impersonal nature of this training.
4. Employees may be too intimidated by the technology or the remoteness of the trainer to ask questions.
5. Lack of computer terminals or insufficient online time may restrict or preclude access to training.
6. Inadequate or outdated hardware devices (e.g., sound cards, graphics accelerators, and local area networks) can cause

programs to malfunction.

7. A company's internet servers may not have enough bandwidth to receive the material.
8. Self-instruction offers limited opportunities to receive context-specific expert advice or timely response to questions.

4.7 Training for Different Employees

Employers are realizing the importance of training. Training allows workers to gain new skills, which improve their work potential. Employers can encourage their employees to stay on their business through workplace training. Skilled workers refer to workers who need specialized training or a learned skill-set to perform a certain task. Skilled workers may be either blue collar or white collar workers. Skilled workers are given training with the help of apprenticeship method of training that may range from one year to five years. Such training is also known as tradesmen or craftsmen. This is useful for such trades in industry which require highly sophisticated skills. Although the mass production in industry has significantly reduced, the proportion of employees who must be skilled tradesmen, electricians, financial technicians, administrative assistants, law enforcement agents and computer operators have increased to such a degree that a very high level of ability and capability is essential to become a skilled tradesman.

Semi-skilled labour also needs a training to face the challenges of an organization arising out of modernization, validation and procedural processes. These employees may be given training either in their own departments or in isolated training shops where machines and other resources are easily available. In this category, training is generally given by skilled employees, employers and inspectors and ranges from few hours to a week. The duration of the training depends upon the contents of a training material. Organizations can use mentorship and coaching method of a training to train employees.

Earlier, unskilled workers did not require special training. But these days, jobs that earlier required little or no training now require training. Training is required to improve performance on a machine, proper handling of material and to do a job in the most economical way. Generally, such workers are given on the job training and training is given by their immediate boss. The time period of this training ranges from 2 weeks to 5 weeks.

The training programme for administrators must be tailor made to fit the needs of an enterprise. A well-trained supervisor is equipped to handle a wide variety of workplace responsibilities in a timely manner. The task of supervisors is to focus upon those areas which are thoroughly connected in their day-to-day activities.

Points to Remember

1. Job rotation is a management approach where employees are shifted from one job to another at regular intervals of time. There are two techniques of job rotation, namely, task rotation and position rotation.
2. Coaching is a kind of daily training and feedback given to the employees by immediate supervisors.
3. The JIT method is a structural method where a trainer prepares a trainee to perform better at the workplace with the help of four steps involving preparation, presentation, performance try out and follow up.
4. Lecture is a verbal presentation of information by an instructor to a large number of employees.
5. Programmed training refers to the subject matter to be learnt in the form of carefully planned sequential units which are often set up through a central panel of an electronic computer as a guide in the performance of a preferred process or series of processes.
6. Conference refers to the holding of a group meeting conducted according to an organized and systematic plan in which members seek to develop knowledge and understanding by getting considerable participation.
7. Simulation involves creating an environment which is similar to real life situations. Simulation technique is widely used in

aeronautical industry.

8. In-basket method is a method where a trainee is required to examine a basket full of papers and files relating to his area of work and make recommendations on problems contained therein.
9. Sensitivity training is an experimental approach to training. It is concerned with making people understand about the behaviour of themselves and others.

Short Answer Type Questions

1. What is the difference between decentralized and centralized training?
2. Define job rotation.
3. What are the characteristics of coaching?
4. Discuss the steps involved in job instruction training.
5. Write down a short note on:

- Programmed training
- Sensitivity training
- E-training
- Conference

6. What is syndicate method?
7. Elaborate any three advantages of simulation.
8. Define vestibule training.
9. What is laboratory training?

Long Answer Type Questions

1. What do you mean by on the job training? Discuss the various methods used in on the job training of employees in an industrial concern.
2. What is computer-based training (CBT)? Explain some important common techniques of CBT.
3. What are the advantages and disadvantages of vestibule training?
4. What are the steps for job instruction training?
5. Enumerate knowledge-based training methods with suitable illustrations.

6. Explain the reasons of employee's priority for apprenticeship programmes? Why are they attractive to organizations?
7. What is the difference between vestibule and simulation training?
8. Discuss the steps of case development. Which aspect of case study do you think is most beneficial for training?
9. Why e-training is becoming popular in organizations these days?
10. Do you think that training methods are helpful to avoid personnel obsolescence? Discuss.

Multiple Choice Questions

Q. 1. Training occurs as a result of

a. Instruction
b. Education
c. Development
d. All of the above

Q. 2. Learning principles do not include

a. Participation
b. Repetition
c. Repatriation
d. Relevance

Q. 3. Which of these is the benefit of needs assessment?

a. Assessment makes training department more accountable
b. Higher training costs
c. Loss of business
d. Increased overtime working

Q. 4. A well-prepared trainer's manual will provide

a. Briefing of training objectives
b. Background of training
c. Everything a trainer needs to know to conduct the training
d. Instructions for the trainer

Q. 5. Which of the following is not a method of on the job training
a. Supervision
b. Job instruction
c. Role play
d. Job rotation

Q. 6. Which of the following is a method of off the job training
a. Supervision
b. Job instruction
c. Role play
d. Job rotation

Q. 7. Which of the following is not a method of off the job training
a. Group discussion
b. Job instruction
c. Role play
d. Case study

Q. 8. Case study method employs
a. Business papers
b. Simulated business problems
c. Actual business situations
d. Real or imaginary roles

Q. 9. One of the demerits of case study method is
a. Lack problem solving scenario
b. One participant can appreciate another's thinking
c. Good case studies do not originate easily
d. Triggers boring debates

Q. 10. Given a case involving an actual company, it is expected
a. To take help of the trainer in every step
b. To consult professional case solvers
c. To give it to your team for review

d. To research the firm to gain a better appreciation of its financial condition and corporate culture

Q. 11. Success of case study method is dependent on
a. The maturity and experience of the trainer
b. Routine handling by the trainer
c. Capability of the trainee to search related topics
d. Use brainstorming approach

Q. 12. Coaching is also known as
a. Feedback
b. Learning by doing
c. Formal training
d. Planned training

Q. 13. Coaching involves
a. Practice and observation
b. Copying the trainer
c. Explaining things why they are so and decision-making meetings with trainees
d. Lecturing

Q. 14. Coaching should be used when
a. An employee is disinterested within the organization
b. An employee is over confident
c. An employee is sufficient enough to do a job skilfully
d. An employee demonstrates a new competency

Q. 15. Job rotation is characterized by
a. Movement of trainee from one location to another
b. Movement of trainee from one job to another
c. Transfer of trainee from one department to another
d. None of the above

Q. 16. Job rotation facilitates
a. General understanding of how the organization functions

b. Providing trainees with specific perspective
c. Limiting the scope of trainees' career
d. Boredom

Q. 17. The problem with job rotation is
a. Trainee cannot handle every kind of situation
b. Trainee is replaced too early
c. Trainee's individual capability is in question
d. Less duration does not develop high degree of expertise in a trainee

Q. 18. One of the merits of job rotation is
a. Workload increases only to an acceptable level
b. The stress produced is minimal
c. Provides valuable opportunities to network within the organization
d. Develops quick learning within few trainees

Q. 19. Apprentices are
a. Trainees who spend a prescribed amount of time working with an experienced guide, coach or trainer
b. Trainees who take lectures from trainer
c. Trainees who are stimulated through actual work conditions
d. None of the above

Q. 20. One important disadvantage of the apprenticeship method is
a. It is only online
b. Uniform period of training offered to trainees
c. Rate of training is uniform
d. None of the above

Q. 21. The method of role play involves
a. Computer-based training with stimulated action behaviour
b. A group cantered approach with everyone doing their own work
c. Method of human interaction that involves realistic behaviour

in imaginary situations
d. Lecture mode

Q. 22. Laboratory training provides trainees with
a. Situations in which trainees' experience themselves through their own interaction
b. Updated technical skills
c. Dummy training session
d. Learner-friendly environment

Q. 23. Which training method is suitable for training clerical and semi-skilled jobs
a. Vestibule training
b. Lecture method
c. Conference method
d. Apprenticeship training

Q. 24. In which training method, trainees are first given background information about a simulated company, its products, pricing etc.
a. In-basked method
b. Simulation
c. Sensitivity training
d. Managerial grid

Q. 25. The abilities developed by in-basked method are
a. Taking participation from group members
b. Understanding group processes
c. Enhanced listening skills
d. Situation judgement in being able to recall details

Q. 26. The main objective of sensitivity training is
a. Arrive at decisions concerning production, pricing etc.
b. Make trainees understand a sample organization
c. Development of awareness of and sensitivity of behavioural patterns of oneself a id others

d. Meeting with several people to discuss the subject of common interest

Q. 27. Sensitivity training results in
a. Little openness with selected people
b. Increased tolerance for individual differences
c. Problem solving
d. Modifies attitudes of trainees

Q. 28. In employee training, last stage for trainee's on the job training is to
a. Present information
b. Prepare learners
c. Do follow up
d. Practice for training

Q. 29. Training which is done through feedback among employees and interactions between co-workers is classified as
a. Informal training
b. Formal training
c. On the job training
d. Off the job training

Q. 30. The method in which 'problem to be solved' is described for employees is called
a. Job rotation
b. Action learning
c. Lifelong learning
d. Case study method

Q. 31. The comparison of on the job behaviour before and after training programme can be classified as
a. Measuring reaction
b. Measuring learning
c. Measuring behaviour
d. Measuring results

Q. 32. A training technique, which allows trainees to solve problems and work in different departments is called

a. Job rotation
b. Action learning
c. Lifelong learning
d. Management development

Q. 33. A systematic method to teach skills for job while presenting facts and getting feedback is called

a. Job rotation
b. Off the job training
c. Job instruction training
d. Programmed learning

Q. 34. The main objective of job instruction technique (JIT) is

a. To make the trainee review every task
b. To train supervisors in the skills of instructing their workers as fast as possible
c. To train employees with theoretical knowledge
d. To make them capable of discussion on a concept

Q. 35. The first step of job instruction technique is to

a. Present the operation
b. Follow up
c. Prepare the worker
d. Try out performance

Q. 36. One of the characteristics of a JIT trainer is

a. Having a time table
b. Conducting group activities
c. Identifying characteristics of how people learn
d. Summarizing a presentation

Q. 37. One of the benefits of job rotation is

a. Reduction in defects
b. Improved safety

c. Create training plans
d. Identification of Knowledge, skills and attitudes required

Q. 38. Which of the following is not a method of job rotation?
a. Departmental attachments
b. Apprenticeship
c. Secondments
d. Understudy assignments

Q. 39. Mentoring is
a. Helping the mentee articulate their dreams, desire and aspirations
b. Actively engaging the participants with work
c. A relationship between an experienced individual and an inexperienced individual where the former provides the training and helps in grooming the latter.
d. Bringing an intellectual change through academic support

Q. 40. Which of the following is not a type of seminar?
a. Main Seminar
b. Mini Seminar
c. Work Seminar
d. National Seminar

Q. 41. Which of the following is not a limitation of seminar?
a. Time liberty
b. Cannot be organized on all the contents of subject matter
c. Limited group discussions
d. Cannot be used for all levels of education

Q. 42. The essence of syndicate method is to
a. Reproduce an actual work setting
b. Facilitate behaviour simulation
c. Necessitate trainees to use some actions
d. Ensure that men learn from each other and contribute their own experience to the fullest

Q. 43. Who is responsible for the relevant documents at the start of a subject in a syndicate method?
a. The Trainee
b. The Chairman and secretary
c. The Trainer
d. The Supervisor

Q. 44. What can one teach in a laboratory method?
a. Chemical safety
b. Critical thinking
c. Troubleshooting
d. Equipment handling

Q. 45. One of the benefits of a lecture method is
a. It is a straightforward way to impart knowledge to students quickly
b. Students with different learning styles will be engaged
c. Students weak in note-taking will remember
d. Teachers will get a real feel on how students understand during lectures

Q. 46. Lectures are preferable
a. To teach skills
b. To enhance cognitive learning
c. To gain straight feedback
d. To transmit information

Q. 47. The main gist of programmed learning is
a. Learning is programmed through computer
b. The trainee directly controls his own learning
c. Interactive reading exercises
d. Encourage self-disclosure and openness

Q. 48. A simulation is
a. Correct visualization of a realistic circumstance
b. Defining objectives of a real life situation

c. A representation of a real life situation with duplicate components of a situation
d. Exploring relationships with another

Q. 49. E-training takes into account the method of
a. Acquiring knowledge and applying that information in potentially unanticipated ways
b. Developing skills in an online environment through speeches, demonstrations and videos
c. Helping employees overcome non-specific issues through internet
d. Continuous training in an inspiring environment

Q. 50. Vestibule training is commonly referred to as
a. Combination of classroom and on the job training
b. Small group achieving a particular purpose
c. Engaging participants by setting up a problem
d. Providing a situation to enact

Answer Key

Q.1.	D	Q.26.	C
Q.2.	C	Q.27.	B
Q.3.	A	Q.28.	C
Q.4.	C	Q.29.	A
Q.5.	C	Q.30.	D
Q.6.	C	Q.31.	A
Q.7.	B	Q.32.	A
Q.8.	B	Q.33.	B
Q.9.	C	Q.34.	A
Q.10.	D	Q.35.	C
Q.11.	A	Q.36.	A
Q.12.	B	Q.37.	D
Q.13.	C	Q.38.	B
Q.14.	D	Q.39.	C
Q.15.	B	Q.40.	C
Q.16.	A	Q.41.	A

Q.17.	D	Q.42.	D
Q.18.	C	Q.43.	B
Q.19.	A	Q.44.	B
Q.20.	B	Q.45.	A
Q.21.	C	Q.46.	D
Q.22.	A	Q.47.	B
Q.23.	A	Q.48.	C
Q.24.	A	Q.49.	B
Q.25.	D	Q.50.	A

5

Management Development Programme

You never change things by fighting the existing reality. To change something, build a new model that makes the existing model obsolete.

—Buckminster Fulle

5.1 Introduction

Managers play an important role in an organization. The success of an organization will depend upon the calibre of a manager in utilizing the resources for achieving an enterprise's objectives. Hence, the outcomes of managerial actions have deep and profound impacts on the entire organization. To lead the race of competition in today's dynamic world, managers need to develop their capabilities that go beyond those required by current the job. Employee development is one of the most important functions of human resource management. Employee development refers to developing and harnessing the abilities of an individual employee and organization as a whole, hence employee development consists of an individual employee and overall growth of the employee as when employees of the organization would develop an organization, organization would flourish more and employee performance would increase (Elena P., 2000). Traditionally, development has focused on management level employees, while line employees received training designed to improve a precise set of skills desired for their current job. However, with the enhanced need to involve employees at different business levels, development is becoming more significant for all employees at all the levels.

Management development programmes are designed to improve the effectiveness of managers and executives not only for the present jobs but also to prepare them for higher level jobs in future. Thus, it is a planned and systematic effort to improve current and future job requirements. The main purpose of a management development programme is to train employees in management skills such as controlling costs, improving efficiency, increase effectiveness and time management. Furthermore, technical training is combined with work experiences to help employees better understand their present job.

Executive development is a systematic process of learning and growth by which employees gain and apply knowledge, skills, and attitude to perform efficiently and competently. It is an education process as it tries to enhance one's ability to understand and interpret knowledge in a useful way.

Few definitions of management development are as under:

Flippo defined management development as, "management development includes the process by which managers and executives acquire not only skills and competency in their present jobs but also capabilities for future managerial tasks of increasing difficulty and scope".

Management Development Institute of India opines, "Management development is the development of management over and above its science and theory, of its practice and application in organizations, corporations and institutions, alike in relation to the organization and manager, so as continuously to re-equip both to fulfil their purposes more effectively and in harmony with each other and both with the environment in which whey function and have their being and hope to thrive upon and grow".

On the basis of above definitions, it can be concluded that management development is a planned, organized and continuous process of learning and growth designed to encourage behavioural change among employees by educating them in order to make them more productive. It is necessary to help managers to keep up with technological developments to build high morale at different levels and to help them create all ideal inter personnel relations in the organization.

5.2 Characteristics of Management Development

The characteristics of management development are as follow:

1. Executive development is a planned and organized process of learning.
2. Executive development helps understand cause and effect of relationship, synthesizes from experience, visualizes relationships or thinks logically.
3. Executive development includes the process by which managers and executives acquire not only skills and competency in their present jobs but also capabilities for future managerial tasks of increasing difficulty and scope.
4. Executive development is a continuous and life-long process. It is not like training as a one-shot programme but an on-going continuous programme throughout the career of an executive or a manager.
5. Fxecutive development is predominantly an educational process rather than a training process.
6. Executive development means not only improvement in job performance, but also enhancement in personality, knowledge, attitude, and behaviourism of an executive.
7. Executive development is based on the assumption that there always exists a gap between what an executive performs and what he/she can. Executive development harnesses this untapped potential.

5.3 Objectives of Management Development

The main objective of management development is to improve the quality of managerial performance. However, other objectives of executive development programme include:

1. To improve managers' performance in their present job.
2. To recognize the employees with the required potential and prepare them for higher positions in future.
3. To ensure accessibility of required number of executives or managers in succession who can take over in case of emergencies as and when these arise in future.

4. To avoid obsolescence of executives by exposing them to latest concepts and techniques in their respective areas of specialization.
5. To develop an environment that is suitable for individual growth.
6. To encourage creativity among the managers.
7. To replace senior executives by highly competent and academically qualified professionals.
8. To increase the versatility of the executives.
9. To help the management to understand the economic, technical and institutional forces in order to solve organizational problems.
10. To improve the thought processes and analytical abilities of the executives.
11. To provide opportunities to executives to fulfil their career aspirations.
12. To recognize the problems of human relations and improve human relation skills.
13. To increase motivation and morale among executives.

5.4 Importance of Management Development

Management development activities help in the growth and improvement of employees. Organizations should nurture their employees to make them feel motivated and develop a sense of loyalty and attachment towards the organization. Employees who give their heart and soul to the organization also expect something in return. Economic benefits could be one motivating factor but nothing like it if an organization prepares its employees not only for his/her current job but also for the future assignments as well. We know technology becomes obsolete with time. An individual needs to keep himself/herself abreast with the latest developments to survive in this fierce competition.

1. **Shortage of Trained Managers**: There is a shortage of trained managers and it is very complicated to recruit and select qualified managerial personnel. Therefore, it becomes necessary for an organization to develop talented and able

employees through a systematic development programme and maintain an inventory of executive skills to meet the future demands of the organization.

2. **Complexity of Management Jobs**: There is noticeable shift from owner managed to professionally managed enterprises, even in family owned business. It has been established that management is a complex job, calling for certain skills, knowledge and attitudes which can only be learnt through systematic development programmes. Due to that, management is now treated as a science and recognized as a distinct branch of knowledge. Management development programmes have been developed by various universities, college and institutes where science as an art of managing people is taught.
3. **Employee Motivation**: Employee development programmes are essential to improve morale and to motivate the employees to perform well. Employees like to learn new skills and meet challenges and they are more motivated when they feel there is great potential for personal growth. When the company shows interest in employee development, the employee naturally has a greater interest in the company's development too.
4. **Technological and Social Changes:** The rapid rate of technological and social changes in society has made it imperative to develop executive talent to cope with these developments. These changes have been brought about by various factors like automation, computers, intense market competition, government controls, awakening of labour, change in the concept of labour etc.
5. **Social Responsibility of Management:** Social responsibility of management has been widely recognized by the business leaders because of the changing social philosophy. Increased management task and leadership responsibilities arising out of social and technological changes has made executive development absolute necessary.
6. **Unending Process:** Executive development is an unending

process. It is not a 'one-shot' affair. It must continue throughout the management career, otherwise an acceptable management of yesterday will not be acceptable today and an executive of today will not be good enough for future. In order to be dynamic and to meet future challenges, a manager should continually educate himself.

It may be concluded that management development programme is absolutely necessary for the success of any organization. No organization can be successful in the long-run without a planned approach to develop its managerial personnel. It is a continuous process to develop the skills of a person and maintain the desired managerial manpower to meet new challenges.

5.5 Key Responsibility of Development

Management development is a strenuous job, which cannot be undertaken by a single department. In order to achieve the development objectives, an involvement of all the departments of an organization is neccssary to integrate development objectives with the organizational objectives. But it is believed that an employee and his immediate superior in an organization is an important key to develop the same. It is a part of every manager's job to develop his employee, as he knows the strengths and weaknesses of his employee. Floyd and Wooldridge (1994) discussed four management roles and strategic thinking:

5.5.1 Championing Strategic Alternatives: Managers play an important part in bringing entrepreneurial and innovative proposals to top management's attention. Championing employs a complex sequence of activities, where first of all, managers proceed as a preliminary screen, choosing a few from the wide range of business prospects, new processes proposals, and administrative innovations suggested at operating levels. Living in the organizational ground between strategy and operations, managers are exclusively capable to make such decisions. In order to pick a proposal, managers begin to cultivate the idea by providing "seed" resources that allow their unit to review the feasibility of an experimental effort.

5.5.2 Synthesizing Information: It refers to supply information to top management about events within and outside the organization. Not all the ideas brought forward by managers are full-blown strategic proposals. Commonly, their role is to supply information to top management concerning internal and external events. They saturate information with meaning through personal evaluation and open advice-giving. Events are likely to be reported as threats or opportunities and these apparently blameless labels are a powerful influence on how superiors come to see their situation. In conveying "facts", managers may be laying the foundation for a future agenda. An opportunity can be championed successfully only when all agree the "timing is right", and usually this requires a considerable amount of prior discussion. Accordingly, middle managers are often able to control, or at least influence, top management perceptions by framing information in certain ways. They are called information filters or "uncertainty absorbers", but the interpretation process is not necessarily conscious or manipulative. In the end, this role can be crucial in encouraging overly cautious top management teams to take the desired risks.

5.5.3 Facilitating Adaptability: Facilitating adaptability concerns with facilitating the change process. Rosa Beth Kanter describes it as the efforts of managers who sheltered and encouraged an employee involvement programme in the midst of an emotional, top-down redesign of production processes. It helps to create an environment in which fears about the change could surface and brought into discussion. Participation helped the organization to adopt new work processes, but the process diverged completely from top management's original intention. Without middle management's efforts to facilitate change, however, the reengineering would have met considerably more resistance and could have failed. Thus, managers are often called change resisters; Kanter describes them as "change masters".

5.5.4 Implementing Deliberate Strategy: Implementing deliberate strategy deals with implementing an organization's strategy. It is pertinent to note that in championing, synthesizing, and facilitating, managers go beyond, or even ignore, the plans implanted in top management's deliberate strategy. The most frequently recognized strategic role of a manager is the implementation of top management's objective. Unsurprisingly, the strategic contribution rests on managers' efforts to organize existing resources efficiently and effectively. There is a widening gap between intentions and implementation. Implementation, therefore, is best characterized as an ongoing series of interventions which are only partly anticipated in top management plans and which adjust the direction to suit emergent events. In short, the conception that top managers formulate strategy while managers carry it out is not only unrealistic; it is also self-defeating. Effective implementation requires that managers have an understanding of the strategic rationale behind the plan, in addition to the specific directives. Such understanding appears to be the result of broad participation in the strategic process, and management's effectiveness in implementing the strategy. The "implementation gap" reflects a broader gap between senior management's perception of implementation, and what managers must know to get the job done.

5.6 Employee Development Plan

Employee development plans prepare an employee for his present as well as future assignments and make him committed and dedicated towards an organization. Employee development plans offers employees the prospect to recognize strengths and development areas that increase their productivity. A good development plan mainly focuses on the development of employee knowledge, develop both strengths and development areas that enhance his performance, and sets gradual, realistic, and achievable success measures. There are two types of employee development plans:

5.6.1 Professional Growth: Professional growth employee development plans are created to help employees in their career growth. In this method, a team manager sits with his team members and designs growth plans with specific deadlines. It is essential to give deadlines to employees for them to take training and employee development activities seriously. Employees should be encouraged to attend training sessions, seminars, and conferences to obtain new skills and knowledge.

5.6.2 Improvement: Organizations design a performance improvement plan to help employees improve their current performance. In this method, employees are trained not only for their professional development but also for their personal growth. Initiatives are taken to improve behavioural skills, communication skills, interpersonal skills which would help them in the long-run.

5.7 Role Playing

A role playing game is a method in which each participant assumes the role of a character, generally in an imaginary or hypothetical situation. It is a classroom exercise in which a number of teams of learners compete with each other to achieve an organizational objective. The main purpose of role playing is to give learners an opportunity to learn human relations skill through practice and to develop insight into one's own behaviour and its effect upon others. Role playing technique is mainly used to develop leadership skill and human skill. Role playing can be used in every department by management and employees to practice business situations.

Role playing is mainly for analyzing problems, developing teamwork, cooperation and creative problem-solving, and improving listening skills. Role playing should be done in a low stress environment, which makes it easier to learn.

The objectives of role playing as a development technique are as under:

1. It helps in increasing a better understanding of the job.
2. It helps in understanding how to handle a particular situation.
3. It helps in developing better understanding of the issue and better decision-making.
4. It helps in anticipating reactions of the other parties.

5. It helps in developing communication, management development and leadership quality.
6. It helps in enhancement of interpersonal relationship.
7. It helps in providing an insight to understanding behavioural patterns of others.

5.8 Special Project

In this method, a trainee may be given a project that is closely related to the objectives of his department. This is a very flexible development device. Such special project assignments grow ordinarily out of an individual analysis of weaknesses. The trainee may be asked to perform special assignment; thereby he learns the work procedure. Sometime a task force is created consisting of a number of learners representing different functions in the organization. The trainee will study the problem, collect the data and analyze it and make recommendations upon it. Learners not only acquire knowledge about the assigned activities, but also learn how to work with others.

5.9 Selective Reading

Individuals in an organization can gather and advance their knowledge and background through selective reading. The reading material can be distributed by the in-charge of executive development programme to the candidates to increase their knowledge and skills. Various business organizations maintain libraries for their own executives. Many executives become members of professional bodies/associations and exchange their ideas with others. This is an excellent method for assimilating knowledge; however, some executives claim that it is very difficult to find time to do much reading other than absolutely required in the performance of their jobs.

5.10 Behaviour Modelling

This is structured approach to teach specific supervisory skills. This is based on the social learning theory in which a trainee is provided with a specific model of behaviour and is informed in advance of the consequences of engaging in that type of behaviour. In this method, some kind of process or behaviour is videotaped and then is watched by the trainees. Games and simulation section is also included because once the trainees see the videotape, they practice the behaviour through role plays or other kinds of simulation techniques. The trainee first observes the behaviour modelled in the video and then reproduces the behaviour on the job. Behaviour modelling includes the following steps:

1. The skills that are required to build up are defined.
2. A brief overview of the theory is then provided to the trainers.
3. Trainees are given instructions that what specific learning points or critical behaviour they have to watch.
4. An expert is used to model the suitable behaviours
5. Trainees are encouraged to practice a suitable behaviour in a role play or through any other method of simulation.
6. Trainees are then provided with some opportunities to give reinforcement for appropriate imitation of the model's behaviour.
7. Trainer ensures that trainees appropriately reinforce the behaviour at the work place.

Behaviour modelling focuses on developing behavioural and interpersonal skills. This type of method can be used for training in:

- Sales training.
- Interviewee training.
- Interviewer training.
- Safety training.
- Interpersonal skills training.

5.11 Special Courses by Universities

In this method, the employers may ask the executives to attend special courses formally organized by the enterprise with the help of experts from educational institutes and universities. The enterprise may also sponsor them to attend certain special courses conducted by professional management bodies. The special courses are gaining popularity now-a-days and many organizations are cond'icting such kind of courses for their employees in order to make them more productive. However, only large enterprises can afford to send their executives to attend such special management development courses conducted by management institutes as the fee charged by them is generally high.

Special courses can be established by business organizations in numerous ways as a part of their development programmes. First, there are courses which the organizations themselves establish to be taught by faculty of the university. Some organizations have regular instructors assigned to their development and development departments such as Tata and Hindustan Lever in the private sector, Life Insurance Corporation, State Bank of India and other nationalized commercial banks, Reserve Bank of India, Hindustan Steel, Fertilizer Corporation and many others in the public sector. A second approach to special courses and lectures is for organizations to work with universities or institutes in establishing a course or a series of courses to be taught by the instructors of these institutes. A third approach is for the organizations to send personnel to programmes established by the universities, institutes and other bodies. Such courses are organized for a short period ranging from 2-3 days to a few weeks.

5.12 Sensitivity Development

Sensitivity development, also known as T-group development, is a type of group development that focuses on helping organizational employees to develop a better awareness of group dynamics and their roles in the group. The development often addresses issues such as gender and multicultural sensitivity as well as sensitivity towards the disabled. The goal of development is focused on individual growth. This method was developed by Kurt Lewin and Ronald Lippitt in 1940. Sensitivity development is sought o increase self-awareness; develop interpersonal competence and sharpen team skills. In this method, the learners are bought together in a free and open environment wherein participants discuss themselves. This method deals with changing behaviour through unstructured group interaction. The sensitivity development programmes are generally conducted under controlled laboratory conditions. The primary focus of this method is on increased openness with others, more concern for others, and increased tolerance for individual differences, less ethnic prejudice, understanding of a group process, enhanced listening skills, and increased trust and support and reducing interpersonal friction by expressing their ideas, belief and attitude.

The activity of a T-group consists mainly of setting around a table discussing for hours. A trainer neither leads the discussion nor suggests what should be discussed but only guides the discussion. The members are encouraged to experiment with their behaviours, offer feedbacks both negative and positive, so that they can change based on the feedback offered. A member can try out new behaviour and can also experience if he/she is more/less satisfied with the new behaviour and its consequences. This development emphasizes on the fact that each of us have an ability to offer solutions to any problems and there need not be a person with authority only to solve problems. It helps bring about confidence in the person to deal with day-to-day problems.

T-group has several characteristic features:

- T-group is normally small, from ten to twenty members.
- The group starts its activity with no formal schedule.
- The role of a trainer is mainly to call thoughts from time to time during the ongoing process within the group.
- The procedure should be inclined to develop introspection and self-examination, with emotional levels of involvement and behaviour and the possibility of colleagues and some breakdown of established insulation and self-defence on the part of individuals.

5.12.1 Purposes of Sensitivity Development: The main purposes of sensitivity development are as follows:

1. Increased understanding, insight, and self-awareness about

one's own behaviour and its impact on others.

2. Increased understanding and sensitivity about the behaviour of others, including better interpretation of both verbal and non-verbal clues, which increases awareness and understanding of what the other person is thinking and feeling.
3. Better understanding and awareness of group and inter-group processes.
4. Increased diagnostic skills in interpersonal and inter-group situations.
5. Increased ability to transform learning into action, so that real life interventions will be more successful in increasing a member's effectiveness, satisfaction, and output.
6. Improvement in an individuals' ability to analyze their own and other's interpersonal behaviour.

5.12.2 Procedures of Sensitivity Development: Sensitivity development programme requires three steps:

1. **Unfreezing the Old Values:** It requires that the learners become aware of the inadequacy of the old values. This can be done when the trainee faces dilemma in which his old values is not able to provide proper guidance. The first step consists of a small procedure:

- An unstructured group of 10-15 people is formed;
- Unstructured group without any objective looks to the trainer for guidance;
- But the trainer refuses to provide guidance and assume leadership;
- Soon, the learners are motivated to resolve the uncertainty;
- Then, they try to form some hierarchy. Some try to assume leadership role which may not be liked by other learners; and
- Then, they started realizing that what they desire to do and realize the alternative ways of dealing with the situation.

2. **Development of New Values:** With the trainer's support, learners begin to examine their interpersonal behaviour and giving each other the feedback. The reasoning of the feedbacks are discussed which motivates learners to

experiment with range of new behaviours and values. This process constitutes the second step in the change process of the development of these values.

3. **Refreezing the New Ones:** This step depends upon how much opportunity the learners get to practice their new behaviour and values at their work place.

5.13 Business Games

Business games are based on a set of rules, regulations, procedures, plans, relationships, and principles derived from research. In this method, trainees are required to gather information, analyze the same and taking effective decisions. Thereafter, the system provides the feedback about the impact of their decisions. Afterwards, on the basis of the feedback they are asked to make decisions again. This process continues until some meaningful results come out or some predefined state of the organization exists or a specified number of trails are completed.

Business games are mainly concerned with skill development of an employee. It helps to stimulate the whole organization and provides a much better perspective than any other training method. This method allows trainees to see how their decisions and actions impact the related areas. There are several methods of business games available. However, they can be broadly classified into two groups, namely, computerized controlled and manual. In computerized controlled, business games are expressed in the form of a mathematical model controlled and manipulated by an electronic computer, while others can be played manually. In computerized controlled games, a quicker feedback is available.

To ensure training and transfer of training, business games used in training should be simple so that trainees can play them in a short period of time. Effective games can produce excitement among the participants and interest in the game. Meaningfulness of the game is improved if it is practical. Trainees need to believe that they are participating in a business and acquiring knowledge, skills, and behaviours that may be useful for the job. Debriefing from a trainer can help trainees understand the game experience and facilitate learning and transfer.

Debriefing can contain feedback, discussions of the concepts obtainable during the game, and instructions in how to use at work the knowledge, skills, or behaviour emphasized in the game. An effective game involves a contest among trainees or teams of trainees or against a recognized measure such as time or quantity. The game is intended to reveal an understanding of or application of a knowledge, skill, or behaviour. Some alternative courses of action are available to trainees, and trainees can guess the consequences of each alternative, but only with some uncertainty.

5.13.1 Objectives of Business Games: The main aims and objectives of a business game are as under:

1. To provide learning and knowledge for better management decision-making in an integrated manner and their implementation.
2. To provide learning of how an organization or industry operates.
3. Helps to categorize interrelationship within the organization.
4. It helps to obtain a better idea and gain gratitude as to how a decision in one organizational unit affects other units.

The merits of this method are as follows:

- It helps to develop leadership skills.
- It improves application of total quality principles.
- It helps in developing skills in using quality tools.
- It strengthens management skills.
- It demonstrates principles and concepts.
- It explores and solves complex organizational problems.

5.14 Seminars

The seminar method is the most modern and advanced method of teaching. Seminars are simply a group of people coming together for a discussion and learning of specific techniques and topics. It is an instructional technique which involves generating a situation for a group to have a guided interaction among themselves on a theme. Usually, there are several keynote speakers within each seminar, and these speakers are usually experts in their own fields, or topics. Several topic reviews are scheduled each day throughout the seminar, and attendees can usually make their choice of topics from among these scheduled events.

Objectives of a seminar are as under:

1. To develop higher cognitive abilities.
2. To develop the ability of responding in a manner that would involve higher cognitive actions.
3. To develop the ability of keen observation of experience and feelings.
4. To develop the ability to seek clarification and defend the ideas of others effectively.

5.15 Action Learning

Action learning is a style of learning in which individuals control their own learning experience, unlike traditional education methods that rely on the development of content by training organizations and delivery by teachers/instructors. Action learning (also known as personal learning) is rapidly gaining popularity among individuals regardless of their stakeholder status such as employees, customers, associates and students. An action learning process includes the following:

1. A real problem that is important, critical, and usually complex.
2. A diverse problem-solving team or "set".
3. A process that promotes curiosity, inquiry, and reflection.
4. A requirement that needs be converted into action and, ultimately, into a solution.
5. A commitment to learning.

Training departments encourage action learning with the help of following:

1. **Formal Collaborative Learning Initiatives:** Collaborative learning is a form of social learning that typically involves groups such as work teams that are formed for discovery-based learning experiences.

2. **Knowledge Repository:** It is an online database that captures, organizes and categorizes knowledge-based information of interest for a specific audience. Knowledge repositories provide a central location for the collection and sharing of digital learning resources.
3. **Personal Learning Environment (PLE):** Personal learning environment is a dedicated internet portal designed to enable learners to manage and control their own learning experiences. This "next generation" web portal, which is not yet in wide use, enables individuals to engage their own personal preferences for formal and informal learning.

5.16 Steps in Management Development Programme

Employee development is an ongoing process which helps employees to enhance their skills and knowledge to contribute more effectively towards an organization. It is essential for employees to upgrade their knowledge with time to survive changing environment and fierce competition at the work place. Employee development process begins from day one when an individual joins an organization. One does not have to wait for annual appraisals to implement an employee development plan. Induction and orienting new employees are also effective ways of employee development.

1. **Looking at Organizational Objectives:** Before deciding to launch a management development programme, it is very important to identify the organizational objectives. The objectives tell "where we are going" and accordingly develop a framework from which executive needs can be determined.
2. **Ascertaining Development Needs:** Next step is ascertaining development needs which requires forecast of needs for present and future growth. This is based upon a comprehensive job analysis with particular reference to the kind of management work performed, the kind of executives needed and the kind of education, experience, development, special knowledge, skills, personal traits, etc., required for such work. It should be clear as to how many and what type

of managers are required to meet the present and future requirements. A comparison of the existing talent with those required to meet the projected needs will help the top management to determine the needs of executive development.

3. **Appraisal of Present Management Talents:** Appraisal of present management talent is made with a view to determining qualitatively the type of personnel available within an organization itself. The performance of a management individual is compared with the standard expected of him. His personal traits are also analyzed so that a value judgment may be made of his potential for improvement. This information helps in disclosing the strength, weaknesses and deficiencies of executives in certain functions relating to the future needs of an organization.
4. **Management Power Inventory:** Management power inventory is prepared for the purpose of getting complete information about each management individual's bio-data and educational qualifications, the results of tests and performance appraisal. From these, it can be known that several capable executives are available for development for higher positions. An analysis of the information will bring to the attention of the management the potential obsolescence of some of the present executives, the inexperience or shortage of managers in certain functions and skill deficiencies relative to the future needs of the organization.
5. **Individual Development Programme:** The planning of individual development programmes in undertaken to meet the needs of different individuals, keeping in view the differences in the attitudes and behaviour, and in their physical, intellectual and emotional qualities. The weak and strong points of an individual are known from his/her performance appraisal reports. On the basis of this information, development programme can be framed and launched.
6. **Establishment of Development Programmes:** After

studying all the above said points, the personnel department can establish a development programme for the employees. A comprehensive and well-conceived programme is prepared; containing concentrated brief courses in different fields, viz. human relations, decision-making, leadership etc.

7. **Evaluating Development Programmes:** Evaluation of development is generally done to obtain information or feedback on the effects of a development programme and assess the value of development. The most important means of evaluating development programmes include observation, ratings, trainee surveys, and trainee interview sets. It is very important to evaluate a development programme as an organization spends lots of resources and money on it. A systematic evaluation of an executive programme will reveal the relevance of the development programme and changes that should be made in order to make evaluation more effective.

Points to Remember

1. Management development programmes are designed to improve the effectiveness of managers and executives not only for the present jobs but to prepare them for higher jobs in future.
2. Employee development plans offers employees the prospect to recognize the strengths and development areas that can enhance their productivity.
3. Employee development plans prepare an employee for his/her present as well as future assignments and make him/her committed and dedicated towards the organization.
4. A role-playing game is a method in which each participant assumes the role of a character, generally in an imaginary or hypothetical situation.
5. Job rotation is a technique where employees are shifted between two or more assignments or jobs at regular intervals of time in order to expose them to all verticals of an organization.

6. Multiple management deals with a permanent advisory board or committee of executives to study the problems of an organization and make recommendations to higher management for final decision.
7. Sensitivity development is also known as T-group development and is a type of group development that focuses on helping organizational employees to develop a better awareness of group dynamics and their roles in the group.
8. Action learning is a style of learning in which individuals control their own learning experience, unlike traditional education methods that rely on the development of content by training organizations and delivery by teachers and instructors.

Short Answer Type Questions

1. Define management development programme.
2. Write a short note on:

a. Management games
b. Special courses
c. Understudy
d. Sensitivity development

3. What is an employee development plan?
4. Discuss the various advantages and disadvantages of job rotation?
5. What are the objectives of role playing?
6. Define behaviour modelling.
7. Discuss the procedure of sensitivity training.
8. What is a business plan?

Long Answer Type Questions

1. What do you mean by management development? Discuss the importance of a management development programme.
2. What are the key responsibilities of development programmes?
3. Explain the steps of a management development programme.
4. Examine the objectives of a management development

programme.

5. "An employee is equally important for employee development". Do you agree?
6. Why management development is necessary in this era?
7. Who is responsible for developing employees?
8. What are the characteristics of a management development programme?
9. Discuss the merits and demerits of sensitivity development.
10. Elaborate various knowledge-based methods of management development programmes.
11. Discuss the types of simulation methods.
12. Why case study method is important for management development? Discuss merits and demerits of a case study method.
13. How action learning can be encouraged in an organization?

Multiple Choice Questions

Q.1 What type of approach is required to make managerial development increasingly effective

a. Thematic approach
b. Reliable approach
c. Systematic approach
d. Learning approach

Q.2 Management development activities are associated with

a. Recruitment
b. Talent management
c. Performance appraisal
d. Organizational structure

Q.3 Training technique which allows trainees to solve problems and work in different departments is called

a. Job rotation
b. Action learning
c. Lifelong learning
d. Management development

Q.4 Training evaluation criteria include all but

a. Relevance
b. Learning
c. Behaviour
d. Results

Q.5 Action learning is particularly effective for

a. Lateral thinking
b. Reflective thinking
c. Solving complex problems
d. Training evaluation

Q.6 Trainer in action learning assists

a. In satisfying leadership training
b. Group members in advancement of their group functioning
c. Trainees to improve their job skills
d. Organization to enhance their value proposition

Q.7 The first step in action learning is

a. Brainstorming
b. Evaluating job behaviour
c. Effective listening
d. Asking questions to clarify the exact nature of the problem

Q.8 Management games were initially devised for

a. Economic variations
b. Organizational effectiveness
c. Military and political decision-making
d. Ultimate value creation

Q.9 A famous management game is

a. Prisoner's Dilemma
b. Corporate Coach
c. Maverick
d. Pacman

Q.10 A training method which targets changing behaviour through unstructured group interaction is called

a. Role play
b. Business games
c. Sensitivity training
d. Behavioural modelling

Q.11 Each management game is based on

a. A more or less realistic model of a business situation
b. Group activity
c. Hypothetical situation
d. None of the above

Q.12 One of the merits of business games is

a. Can learn about the development of business games
b. Compresses time
c. Promotes overview of a real situation
d. Not expensive to develop

Q.13 Understudy is a method that supplies the organization a

a. Person with high networking
b. A person who can act as an instructor
c. Person with as much competence as the superior to fill his post
d. Person who can be a role model

Q.14 Understudy helps in an opportunity to learn

a. New techniques and tools
b. Job knowledge
c. Market knowledge
d. The superior's job and get ready for challenging roles at a later date

Q.15 Seminars are organized by

a. Companies and universities
b. Professional associations

c. Specialized consultants
d. All of the above

Q.16 University related programs utilize
a. Cases and lectures to provide management skills
b. Interviewing process
c. Management games
d. Role plays

Q.17 The first step in behavioural modelling is
a. Role playing
b. Social reinforcement
c. Modelling
d. Transfer of training

Q.18 In social reinforcement the trainer
a. Gives feedback
b. Provides reinforcement in the form of praise and constructive feedback
c. Encourages trainees to apply their new skills
d. Makes trainees watch live or videos showing models

Q.19 In a multiple management system
a. Trainees acquire knowledge of one aspect of business
b. Helps to identify the members who lack the skills of a manager
c. There is no group interaction
d. Permanent advisory committees of managers study problems of the company and make recommendations to higher management

Q.20 Multiple management system is also called
a. Committee system
b. Junior board of executives system
c. Superior board of executives system
d. General management system

Answer Key

Q.1.	B	Q.11.	A
Q.2.	A	Q.12.	B
Q.3.	B	Q.13.	C
Q.4.	A	Q.14.	D
Q.5.	A	Q.15.	D
Q.6.	B	Q.16.	A
Q.7.	D	Q.17.	C
Q.8.	C	Q.18.	B
Q.9.	A	Q.19.	D
Q.10.	C	Q.20.	B

6

Evaluation: Meaning and Significance

A truthful evaluation of yourself gives feedback for growth and success.

—Brenda Johnson Padgitt

6.1 Introduction

Organizations spend huge money and resources on training and development of employees hence it is necessary to determine its effectiveness in terms of achievement of the training objectives. Not only organizations, but employees also like to know how much they have learnt or how well they are doing. Consequently, it is very pertinent to examine a training programme. The process of examining a training programme is called training evaluation. Training evaluation is a continual and systematic process of assessing the potential value of a training programme, course, contents or activities involved in the training programme. Training evaluation checks whether training has had the desired effect on the trainees or organizations or not. Organizations are required to evaluate their training programmes constantly to determine how well such programmes contribute to mission accomplishment and meet organizational performance. Employees like to know how much they have learnt or how well they are doing.

Evaluation of a training programme is the last stage of a training and development process. It is not only for an organization, trainer, instructor and evaluator, but it is also absolutely vital for the learner or the trainee. Hence, it is very important for an organization to evaluate individuals properly, fairly and with as much support as the environment allows. Training evaluation can help an organization to achieve many different goals during the life cycle of a training programme.

Training evaluation is an effective tool to understand the returns that training produces and gives information desired to improve training. If an organization receives an inadequate return on its investment in training, the organization will likely decrease its investment in training or look for training providers outside an organization who can provide training experiences that improve employee performance, satisfaction, morale, productivity, motivation, customer satisfaction, or whatever other outcomes the organization is keen in accomplishing. Reasons for doing an evaluation of training include:

1. It recognizes the importance of satisfying the needs of clients.
2. It provides justification for the investment in training.
3. It establishes the benefits of having a training function.
4. It encourages management to make further investment in training.
5. It enables training to be valued from different perspective.
6. It includes cost-benefit analysis.
7. It provides professional discipline for training management.
8. It encourages careful scrutiny of the training proposals.

But in reality, organizations, managers and trainers at high levels are too busy worrying about profits, return on investment, stock prices, and other matters of concern to the board of directors, stockholders, and customers. They pay little or no attention to training unless they hear bad things about it. As long as trainees are happy and do not complain, trainers feel comfortable, relaxed, and secure. However, if trainees react negatively to the programmes, trainers begin to worry, because the word might get to the higher level managers that the programme is a waste of time or even worse and higher level managers consequently might make decisions based on this feedback.

6.2 Definitions

Few definitions of training evaluation are as under:

Ralph Tyler defined "evaluation as a process of determining to what extent the educational objectives are being realized".

Hamblin defined training evaluation as "an attempt to obtain information (feedback) on the effects of training programme and to assess the value of training in the light of that information for improving further training".

Phillips defined evaluation "as a systematic process to determine the worth, value or meaning of something".

On the basis of the above definitions, it can be concluded that training evaluation is a repetitive, systematic and organized process of assessing the effectiveness of a training programme done by collecting data on whether the participants were satisfied with the deliverables of the training programme and whether they learnt something from the training and are able to apply those skills at their workplace.

6.3 Types of Training Evaluation

There are many types of evaluation depending on what is being evaluated and the purpose of the evaluation. Perhaps the most important basic distinction in evaluation types is formative, summative, process and output evaluation.

6.3.1 Formative Evaluation: A formative evaluation usually takes place during the early stages of a training programme and addresses questions about implementation and ongoing training planning. The purpose of formative evaluation is to validate or ensure that the goals of the training programme are being achieved and to improve the instructions, if necessary, by means of identification and subsequent remediation of problematic aspects.

6.3.2 Summative Evaluation: Summative evaluation assesses the outcomes or impacts of a training programme. It helps to determine the relationship of different factors to outcomes. Similar to formative evaluations, some information used in summative evaluations is collected early in the life of a programme (e.g., baseline data, test scores). The main purpose of summative assessment is to evaluate employee learning at the end of a training programme by comparing it against some standard or benchmark.

6.3.3 Process Evaluation: Process evaluation documents the process of a training programme's implementation. Training process implementation helps stakeholders see how a training programme outcome or impact was achieved. It is typically done at the end of the training and it looks at the programme from start to finish, assessing cause-and-effect relationships between the training components and the outcomes.

6.3.4 Output Evaluation: Outcome evaluations assess the effectiveness of a training programme in producing change. Outcome evaluations focus on difficult questions that ask what happened to training participants and how much of a difference the training made for them. Outcome evaluations are undertaken when it is important to know whether and how well the objectives of a training project or programme were met.

6.4 When Should Training be Evaluated in an Organization?

It is quite obvious that training is evaluated at the end of a training session. It is not possible to evaluate training after every course. These programmes should be evaluated to determine whether they should be continued or not. If the cost outweighs the benefits, the programme should be discontinued or modified. Validation is an effective phenomenon to let the trainer know that the contents has not wandered off track and are still delivering the required standards. Another time evaluation is required when there has been a significant change or when the course is due to be revised or replaced by a new course. Evaluation of training also occurs annually when an organization is assessing the success of its business plan. Evaluating a training programme at the end of a training session can help answer the following questions in a better way:

1. To what extent does the subject content met the needs of those attending?
2. Is the leader the one best qualified to teach?
3. Did the leader use the most effective methods for maintaining interest and teaching the desired attitudes, knowledge, and skills?

4. Are the facilities satisfactory?
5. Is the schedule appropriate for the participants?
6. Are the aids effective in improving communication and maintaining interest?
7. Was the coordination of the programme satisfactory?
8. What else can be done to improve the programme?

A careful analysis of the answers to these questions can identify ways and means of evaluating a training programme. There are many companies, which are using reaction sheets (such as smiles). But there are many companies which avoid using reactions sheets because of one or more of the following reasons:

1. They do not consider it important or urgent.
2. They do not know what to do or how to do it.
3. There is no pressure from top management to do more.
4. They feel secure in their job and see no need to do more.
5. They have too many other things that are more important.

6.5 Principles of Evaluation

Evaluation plays an integral part of a training system meant to aid trainers/training managers to plan and adjust their training activities in an attempt to increase the prospect to accomplish the desired action or goals. Employee performance and learning can be observed and measured. Line managers, in partnership with trainees, and top level management and community, are accountable for ensuring improvement in employee achievements. Effective training evaluation systems promote improvement of professional practice resulting in improvement of employee performance. An effective training evaluation system includes the following principles:

1. Evaluator should be clear about the purpose of evaluation to be capable to set the principles and criteria of evaluation.
2. Evaluation should be a never ending process. It deals with continuously identifying the problems and solving them by taking necessary steps. It is an ongoing process.
3. The methodology and criteria of evaluation should be based on recognizable and as far as possible measurable standards

of assessment which have been decided upon by the evaluators and the users of the training system.

4. The training objectives should be a result of overall organizational goals to allow tangible evaluation of training results.
5. Evaluation should be directive rather than conclusive. It must be comprehensive enough to direct evaluator in the collection of information that will enable them to observe efficacy of current training programme and to improve upon subsequent training programmes.
6. A good evaluative system should offer adequate scope for self-assessment by the trainer/evaluator.
7. A good evaluation system is tailor-made and should provide specific data about its strength and weaknesses. Generalizations drawn from one training activity may be inapplicable for training across different levels and to meet different standards. Besides, they should refrain from using single instances for conclusions and generalizations.
8. Evaluator should set realistic targets. A sense of urgency no doubt is desirable but deadlines that are idealistically high will result in inappropriate quality.
9. Reporting system of evaluative data should be easy, apparent, sufficient and accessible.
10. Evaluator should be tactful and honest.
11. Efficient communication and harmonization are important for training evaluation. Evaluator should discuss evaluation plans with trainers, evaluators and top level management.

6.6 Five Levels of Training Evaluation

Evaluation of training effectiveness is one of the essential aspects of training and development. Without proper evaluation of the effectiveness of training and development activities, it will be impossible to determine how well the training programme will achieve its objectives. Phillips advocates the following five levels of evaluation.

6.6.1 Reaction: Reaction relates to the feeling of the

participants about training and training methods. Training reactions are typically measured at the end of training. However, that is a summative or end of course assessment and reactions are also measured during the training, even if only informally in terms of the instructor's perception.

Trainee's reaction to the overall effectiveness of a training programme includes content of the subject matter, time taken by each topic, method of training, and intellect level of the trainer, which is helpful in determining the effectiveness of the training programme. It brings all the trainees upon a level of knowledge and experience. It is subjective rather than objective, because every participant is free to react in his/her own way.

6.6.2 Learning: The change in a participant's knowledge and skills carried out by the implementation of a training programme is essential in order to evaluate the effectiveness of training. The effectiveness of a training programme is measured on the basis of a trainer's ability by asking different questions, the duration of the training programme and learner's ability to apply that knowledge to the job. It addresses the question: Did the participants learn anything? Learning evaluation requires post-testing, so that an evaluator can differentiate between what they already knew prior to the training and what they actually learnt during the training programme. If the participants are imparted with specific knowledge and skills, the training is said to be effective.

6.6.3 Behaviour: It is an important while evaluating a training programme, to determine the extent to which trainee has applied his/her knowledge and skills towards his/her job. Evidently, any evaluation of changes in on the job behaviour must take place in the job environment only. The level of behaviour is defined as the degree to which a change in behaviour has arisen because the participant attended the training programme. This evaluation involves testing the trainee's capabilities to perform learnt skills back on the job.

6.6.4 Affective Outcomes: Affective outcomes indicate attitudes, values, discipline, thinking, communication and motivation of the trainees. These outcomes are expected to occur through informal learning. Affective outcomes that might be collected in an evaluation comprise of tolerance for diversity, belief to learn, motivation to learn, safety attitudes, and customer service orientation. Affective outcomes can be measured with the help of surveys and observations. Proper implementation of affective domain can boost learning and can even influence cognitive learning. Affective learning is often contrasted with cognitive learning, which is associated with synthesis, evaluation, and comprehension of knowledge or information.

6.6.5 Result: It is another useful criterion of evaluating training effectiveness. This evaluation measures the reaction, learning and change in job behaviour of the trainee in the form of enhanced performance, job satisfaction, motivation, morale and productivity. When an individual shows a different method of performing a job after attending a training programme, it is assumed that the training has been effective. It measures the training effectiveness for an organization by answering the following questions:

- What impact has the training achieved?
- Is it working and yielding value for the organization?
- Is it providing monetary benefits to the organization?
- Does it help to increase the effectiveness of the organizations?

These questions mainly reflect the impact of the programme in an organization in the form of monetary benefits, efficiency, morale, team behaviour, turnover etc.

Evaluation criterion indicates improvement in overall performance of organizational activities. The ultimate value of contribution of a training programme to an organization may be measured in the form of growth, performance, goodwill, profitability etc. and to the individual in the form of personality development, job satisfaction, self-development etc. Hence, a training programme should be organized on these aspects of organizational performance. Training seems to be effective only if it achieves its stated goals and objectives.

6.7 Purposes of Evaluation of a Training Programme

The main purpose of training and development evaluation is to determine the effectivencss of a programme and ways in which it can be improved. These training and development programmes should be evaluated to determine whether they should be continued or not. If the cost outweighs the benefits, the programme should be discontinued or modified. Some additional purposes include the following:

1. Assessing how much of the knowledge, expertise and skills learnt during the training programme by trainees.
2. Gathering information about inputs, contents, course, activities and outcomes.
3. Determining the postulation upon which an existing or proposed training course or programme is based.
4. Inquiring up front, about the expected results.
5. Comparison of post-training outcome with pre-set standards or targets.
6. Measuring whether the results of the training programme contributed to the achievement of the organization's goals.
7. Reporting result in a manner that facilitates their use and improves programme effectiveness.
8. To appraise the status of and changes in trainee's behaviour.
9. To make provision for guiding the growth of an individual trainee.
10. To diagnose an individual trainee's educational weakness and strength.
11. To predict a trainee's future professional success.
12. To provide basis for modification of curriculum and courses.
13. To locate areas where remedial measures are needed.
14. To provide basis for the introduction of experiences to meet the needs of individuals and group of trainees.
15. Motivate trainees towards better attainment and growth.
16. To test the efficiency of trainer.
17. Appraise the trainer, instructor and supervisors' competence.
18. Improve instructions, measurements and measuring devices of training.

19. Bring out the inherent capabilities of a trainer, such as attitudes, habits, appreciation and understanding, and manipulative skills in addition to conventional acquisition of knowledge.

6.8 Steps of Training Evaluation

Training evaluation allows an organization to achieve continuous improvement in the training process.

1. **Establish Standards:** It is important that organizations should develop a set of standards and these standards will allow an organization to evaluate the different aspects of a training programme in relation to the best practices and industry standards. Standards are powerful tools for change when they are aligned with an institution's mission and strategic objectives. Programme benchmarks can be based on initial trainee's training requirements, government accreditation, comparative analyses and employer needs. This comprehensive set of standards then becomes the baseline from which an organization will monitor its progress.
2. **Identify Stakeholders:** Training affects a variety of stakeholders, so it is very important to involve them in training evaluative process. Training evaluation moves beyond simply administering programme to trainees and includes gathering feedback from a wide array of stakeholder groups. Training programme stakeholders can be classified into three main categories: those served by the training programme, those involved in training operations and those who will use the training evaluation data. All of these audiences must be engaged in the training process so that a comprehensive view of the training programme is established. The multi-source feedback in assessment will provide the organisation with useful and diverse feedback for continual training programme improvement.
3. **Describe the Training Programme:** The next step in the training evaluation process is to describe the training programme that will be evaluated. The programme

description plays an important role as it becomes a reference for all future training programme decisions. This description should include the training programme's goals, objectives, learning outcomes, training structure and how it fits into the overall learning environment. The summary should also include a list of resources and activities that are needed to accomplish the training programme's goal. It is important that the programme description be agreed upon by all training stakeholders. If there is no clear and accepted description the evaluation runs risk of producing inaccurate and questionable data.

4. **Design the Evaluation:** In a training evaluation, an organization should determine the purpose of the training evaluation and its design. The purpose of training evaluation can be to measure trainee learning, find ways to improve the programme or to determine the programme's effectiveness. Training evaluations can focus on a variety of areas such as processes, resources, activities and outcomes of training. It is also very important for the organization how to use the information and what are the best methods for collecting feedback in the organization. Establishing a proper training purpose and method will help the organization in evaluating the training programme. Training evaluation questions can be based on: an institution's training mission, the programme's goals and objectives, previous training needs assessments, training strategic plans, training accreditation criteria, etc.
5. **Collect Feedback:** In this stage of training evaluation, an organization needs to determine the type of data they want to collect and the appropriate evaluation method. The data an organization obtains may be qualitative or quantitative, depending on their needs. The type of data they compile will depend on the training questions they design and the target audience. Depending on the training audience, an organization may use qualitative feedback methods such as interviews, focus groups or observation. For a different audience, they may collect quantitative data regarding the

training programme. Organizations can achieve this by methods such as surveys and questionnaires. Regardless of the method, organizations will have to take great care to ensure that the information is valid and reliable.

6. **Analyze Results:** The last step involves analyzing the results. In this step, an organization can look for trends, gaps, strengths and areas for improvement in the data to get a picture of how the training programme is performing. While analyzing, an organization needs to interpret the significance of the training results and consider different ways to compare the data. At this point of time, an organization will have to go back to the standards and programme descriptions and compare the information. This will allow the evaluator to understand if a training programme is meeting its objectives, goals and learning outcomes. As a part of the training analysis phase, recommendations should be provided that are consistent with the findings. These recommended actions or decisions will form the basis for any training programme alterations.
7. **Make Improvements:** In this stage, an evaluator will share the training evaluation report and recommendations with relevant stakeholders. These decision-makers will play an integral role in deciding if the training programme improvements or alterations were implemented. The recommendations, along with stakeholder input, will drive which actions get implemented and when. Training programme changes can range from small improvements in the curriculum to strategic decisions such as ending the programme. Regardless of the actions, an evaluator needs to ensure that all aspects are considered such as impact, policy implications and budget. He should keep in mind that follow-up may be necessary to remind stakeholders of the agreed-upon actions to ensure improvements get executed.
8. **Continuous Monitoring:** Continuous monitoring should be an integral part throughout the evaluation process. An evaluator should make regular improvements in the

programme, regularly monitors it and compares it to the initial standards. This frequent monitoring will help the evaluator that the programme provides a consistently high return on expectations. It is defined as a "framework of holistic measures of the training benefits that are realized from any training programme or initiative, both qualitative and quantitative".

6.9 Guidelines for Planning an Effective Training Evaluation Process

Interestingly, it is not just the implementation phase that needs to follow best practices. To ensure the success of a training evaluation process, the planning of an effective training evaluation process should also follow some effective guidelines. Following points will review six planning guidelines to help evaluators to achieve an effective training course or training evaluation process.

1. **Clearly Determine the Purpose of the Training Evaluation:** First of all, the evaluator must determine the purpose of the training evaluation. He should determine if he/she is looking to assess the quality of the course, the effectiveness of the instructor or the experience of the trainee? He/she should be sure to communicate the purpose to all stakeholders involved in the training process. Further, an evaluator needs to decide how the training feedback will be utilized in an organization.
2. **Establish the Focus of the Evaluation:** The evaluator should establish the focus of the evaluation. The focus could be on the training curriculum and materials, the training approach or on trainee engagement and learning outcomes. Evaluator should be sure that the questions reflect the stated purpose and goal.
3. **Determine the Target Audience:** Often, evaluations are completed by trainees. However, some instructors desire a broader view and select colleagues to also review the quality of their training. The purpose and focus of training evaluation

should align with the audience and the questions should be tailored accordingly.

4. **Create Policies and Procedures:** This is where an organization can determine the roles and responsibilities of those involved in the training process (trainer, instructors, system administrators, etc.). Training procedural document will also include details on who will see the training evaluation results and who is responsible for acting upon the training feedback. He should be sure to include clear policies on confidentiality.
5. **Utilize Multiple Sources and Methods of Evaluation:** To get an overall and balanced view of the evaluation, an evaluator should include trainees, peer and self-evaluation. The use of multiple sources of feedback gives a sound basis for development opportunities and personnel decisions. Multiple methods can include online evaluations, interviews, observations, etc. It is also important to include ongoing trainee's feedback by implementing early and/or mid-term evaluation.
6. **Conduct Training Sessions:** Organizations should conduct training sessions for all involved. It is important to train all stakeholders in the evaluation process including policies and procedures and how to use the online system (set-up and reports). Separate training or information sessions will be needed for administrators, instructors and trainees. Trainers that use the feedback for decision-making purposes will also need to be trained on how to interpret and use ratings.

6.10 Implication of Evaluating a Training Programme

Evaluators generally look for validity, accuracy, and reliability in their training evaluation system.

6.10.1 Before Training: Before the training programme, an analysis is conducted to identify what areas of knowledge, skill and behaviour is required to accomplish with the learner. The before training analysis considers what results the organization needs from the trainer, what knowledge and skills the learner presently has and usually concludes with identifying what knowledge and skills the learner must gain (the "performance gap"). During the start of training, candidates generally perceive it as a waste of resources because at most of the times candidates are unaware of the objectives and learning outcomes of the programme.

Once aware, they are asked to give their opinions on the methods used and whether those methods confirm to the candidate's preferences and learning style. Usually, this phase also includes identifying when training should occur and who should attend as learners. Ideally, a criteria is established for the final evaluation of training to conclude if training goals were met or not.

Depending on the resources and needs of the organization, a before training stage can range from a very detailed inventory of skills to a general review of performance results. The more complete the training analysis, the more likely that an employee's training will ultimately contribute results to the organization.

It may be pointed out that employees require training for a variety of reasons, which usually fall into two categories:

1. Training to fill a "performance gap" as identified during the performance management process.
2. Training to fill a "growth gap", that is to use it for promotion or be able to fill another open position in the organization.

6.10.2 During Training: It is this phase, in which instructions are given. Trainees should be continually assessed during the training programme to determine any problems and ensure that they are given every opportunity to develop the required skills. At the same time, identification of problems encountered by a trainee will indicate weaknesses in the training programme and/or the ability of the trainer to implement the programme. All tests used to assess trainees' abilities must be relevant and reliable. During training, an evaluator should focus on the following:

1. The trainer needs to help the trainees to become "self-learners", i.e. they learn by themselves, independent of a

trainer, using books and experience.

2. Trainees need to be numerated to allow them to make simple calculations and keep records. The trainer needs to incorporate arithmetic into the course to ensure that trainees are capable of performing the simple mathematical calculations deemed necessary in their work.
3. Periodically conduct a short test.
4. Are they able to divide the complex task into a simpler one? After some experience the trainer will be able to tell whether any of the objectives need to be changed or omitted, whether it is necessary to make new objectives, and if the assessment tests are satisfactory. He will also be able to judge whether the training conditions are satisfactory or will need to be changed. In this way, the trainer will be able to improve upon the programme.
5. Is the trainee enthusiastically taking part in interacting with others? Trainees need to develop the ability to listen respectfully to others, to encourage them to talk about their problems. A trainee needs to deal respectfully but firmly with team members and the elders and leaders of the team. Trainees will also need to be able to determine what is important and what is not and develop the skills of persuading people to do what is necessary to improve the functioning of the organization.

6.10.3 After Training: It is a phase when learner's knowledge, skills and learning are assessed again to measure the effectiveness of the training programme. This phase is designed to determine whether training has had the desired effect on an employee's performance and organizational objectives. To evaluate the training effect, the following criteria can be used:

1. An evaluator can give him/her the test before and after training and development, and compare the results of the candidate?
2. He can observe his/her behaviour at the workplace.
3. He can interview him or her before and after and compare the results?

Following guidelines should be kept in mind while evaluating a participant after the training programme:

1. To what extent, training needs objectives have been achieved by the programme?
2. To what extent were the learner's learning objectives achieved?
3. What specifically did the learners learnt or be usefully reminded off?
4. To what extent were they supported in this?

6.11 Parties Involved in Training Evaluation

There are numerous different parties that should be involved in training evaluation and those are presented below.

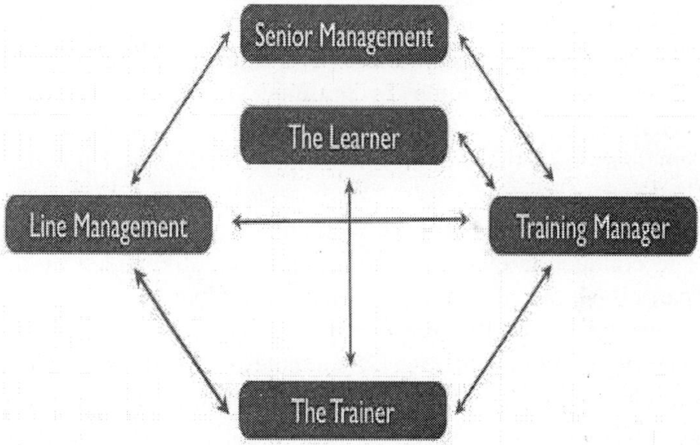

The Evaluation Quintet by **Leslie Rae**, taken from 'Assessing the Value of Your Training' **(2002)**

6.11.1 Senior Management: Senior management should encourage managers to allocate appropriate resources for evaluating a training programme. An organization should be aware of the needs and values of training to an organization. Top management should also be influential in driving change as a consequence of training evaluation outcomes. As we know that since they have busy schedules, however, they should be actively involved in presenting information in a way that enables them to quickly assimilate those training outcomes. They must focus on the necessity of involving the training manager in senior management meetings where decisions are made about future changes when training will be essential.

6.11.2 Training Manager Contribution: Training manager plays an important role in ensuring that training evaluation occurs properly within the organization. Training manager is the architecture of a training programme. He should interface with senior managers over evaluation results as well as engaging with line managers on how they can support and inform a training evaluation process. The introduction and maintenance of evaluation systems and production of regular reports for senior management is the foremost responsibility of a training manager. Training managers must liaison with the line managers in assessment of the training programme. He must focus on maintenance of interest and support in the planning and implementation of the training programme, including a practical involvement.

6.11.3 Line Manager: Involving line managers is essential in order to conduct an evaluation. It is highly recommended by the Kirkpatrick Model of training evaluation. As we know that line managers are generally busy people, it is up to the training manager to communicate why their role is so important in a training programme and they hold significant influence over how effectively training can be transferred into the workplace. Line managers should be encouraged to participate in determining what type of evaluation activity occurs for different types of training. They can give ongoing and practical support to the training programme. They should hold a debriefing meeting with the learners on their return to work to discuss, agree or help to modify and agree for an action plan.

6.11.4 The Trainer: Trainers are quite crucial in training evaluation process. Individual trainers need to be made aware of the methodologies that are to be used to evaluate training. In a training environment, trainers can influence to a large extent and should attempt to create an environment where participants feel that they would be able to provide an open and honest feedback. They will also be integral as to how the participants are assessed and will need to be clear about the assessment procedures to ensure they are applied consistently. Trainers will need to be provided with the results of the training evaluation so that they can be involved in developing and implementing any necessary action plans.

6.11.5 The Learner: Finally the learner, as well as having the zeal to learn, also needs to contribute to the training evaluation process. Although the principle role of the learner in the programme is to learn, but the learner also must be involved in the evaluation process. This is important, since without their comments much of the evaluation could not occur. Learners need to provide their initial feedback on training, undertake assessments at the end of training and provide their views on the relevance and opportunity to transfer learning into the workplace after the training programme. There must be an involvement of the learner in the planning and design of the evaluation process. Without this interaction, the process will lack the foundation data upon which the evaluation results will be formed. For learners to neglect either of the responsibilities, an organization wastes its investment in a training programme. Learners will assist more readily if the process avoids the look and feel of a paper-chase or number-crunching exercise.

Points to Remember

1. Training evaluation is a continual and systematic process of assessing the potential value of a training programme, course, contents or activities involved in a training programme. Training evaluation checks whether training has had the desired effects on trainees and organizations or not.
2. There are four types of evaluation viz. formative evaluation, summative evaluation, process evaluation and output evaluation.

3. Phillips advocates five levels of evaluation and those five levels include reaction, learning, behaviour, results and evaluation.
4. The main purpose of training and development evaluation is to determine the effectiveness of a programme and ways in which it can be improved. These training and development programmes should be evaluated to determine whether they should be continued or not.
5. Training evaluation allows organizations to achieve continuous improvement in the training process. Training includes establishing standards, identifying stakeholders, describing the training programme, designing evaluation, collecting feedback, analyzing results, and continuous monitoring.
6. The main parties involved in training evaluation programme include senior managers, training managers, line managers, trainers and learners.

Short Answer Type Questions

1. Define training evaluation?
2. What do you mean by formative evaluation?
3. Discuss the various types of training evaluation.
4. Define the following terms:

- Learning
- Behaviour
- Reaction

5. Name the parties involved in evaluation of a training programme.

Long Answer Type Questions

1. What do you understand by training evaluation? Describe the steps in training evaluation.
2. What are the objectives of training evaluation?
3. Explain the implications of training evaluation in modern organizations.
4. What can be done to inspire organizations to evaluate training

programmes?

5. Define formative evaluation. What is the difference between formative and summative evaluation?
6. What are the principles that should be kept in mind while evaluating a training programme?
7. Discuss the various guidelines for planning an effective training programme.

Multiple Choice Questions

Q.1 Training evaluation criteria include all but

a. Relevance
b. Learning
c. Behaviour
d. Results

Q.2 Concept of four level training evaluation (reaction, learning, behaviour and results) was advocated by

a. Donald Kirkpatrick
b. Robert Mathis
c. John
d. None of the above

Q.3 In training evaluation, measurement of how much of concepts, attitudes and theories learnt that has made an impact on job is classified

a. Learning evaluation step
b. Behaviour evaluation step
c. Reaction evaluation step
d. Results evaluation step

Q.4 In training evaluation, measurement of training effect on performance and observation of job performance is classified as

a. Reaction evaluation step
b. Results evaluation step
c. Learning evaluation step
d. Behaviour evaluation step

Q.5 In training evaluation, measurement of training effect on performance and observation of job performance is classified as

a. Reaction evaluation step
b. Results evaluation step
c. Learning evaluation step
d. Behaviour evaluation step

Q.6 Which of the following is a benefit to the individual while receiving training

a. Creates an appropriate climate for growth, communication
b. Aids in increasing productivity and/or quality of work
c. Satisfies personal needs of a trainer
d. None of the above

Q.7 Which of the following is a technique of evaluation

a. Longitudinal or time series analysis
b. Transfer validity
c. Inter-organizational validity
d. None of the above

Q.8 Evaluation helps determine the extent to which ________have been achieved

a. Efficiency
b. Profit
c. Training objectives
d. Employee satisfaction

Q.9 Evaluation gives insights for

a. Reviewing
b. Adjusting
c. Revising goals
d. All of the above

Answer Key

Q.1.	A
Q.2.	A

Q.3.	A
Q.4.	D
Q.5.	D
Q.6.	B
Q.7.	A
Q.8.	C
Q.9.	D

7

Training Evaluation Models

Solutions to problems are like keys in locks; they don't work if they don't fit. And if solutions aren't the right ones, the problem doesn't get solved.

—R. Mager and P. Pipe

Training evaluation models is a systematic approach that will guide in measuring the efficiency and effectiveness of a training, a course or an educational program. Evaluation models goals involves multiple purposes including evaluation of learning, evaluation of instructional material, transfer of training, return on investment and so on. The details of the various evaluation models used in training are discussed below.

7.1 Kirkpatrick Model of Training Evaluation

Donald Kirkpatrick first published his idea in 1959, in a series of articles in the US Training and Development Journal. The model was then updated in 1975, and again in 1994, when he published his best-known work, "Evaluating Training Programs". The model has gained international acclamation and is now considered as a standard across the HR and training communities. The focus is on measuring four kinds of outcomes that should result from a highly effective training program. Kirkpatrick's four levels are designed as a sequence of ways to evaluate training programs. Many practitioners believe that as you proceed through each of the levels, evaluation becomes more difficult and requires more time. Kirkpatrick's model includes four levels and steps of outcome evaluation.

The four levels of Kirkpatrick's evaluation model are as follows:

1. **Reaction:** What participants thought and felt about the

training (satisfaction; "smile sheets").

2. **Learning:** The resulting increase in knowledge and/or skills, and change in attitudes. This evaluation occurs during the training in the form of either a knowledge demonstration or a test.
3. **Behaviour:** Transfer of knowledge, skills, and/or attitudes from classroom to the job (change in job behaviour due to training program). This evaluation occurs 3-6 months post training while the trainee is performing in the job. Evaluation usually occurs through observation.
4. **Results:** The final results that occurred because of attendance and participation in a training program (can be monetary, performance-based, etc.)

7.1.1 Advantages of Evaluating a Reaction: These are as under:

1. It helps to know how the participants felt about the training event.
2. It may point out areas that trainees felt were missing from the training event.
3. It will tell you how engaged the participants felt by the training event.
4. It can provide information about overall participant reaction as well as participant feedback and evaluation of specific aspects of the training event.
5. Detailed level one evaluation can provide formative evaluation information that can be used to improve future versions of the training program.

7.2 CIPP Evaluation Model

CIPP model of programme evaluation was advanced by Daniel L. Stufflebeam (1983). CIPP model is a management oriented evaluation designed to provide definitive and valid information for decision-makers in typical business-minded, managerial type position, though taking into account the diverse levels of decision and decision-makers. CIPP deals with four phases of evaluation: context evaluation, input evaluation, process evaluation and product evaluation. It is grounded upon the view that the most important purpose of evaluation is to increase the functioning of a programme.

The objectives of process evaluation are as under:

1. To provide feedback to the organizations and their employees about the extent to which the activities are on schedule and are being carried out as planned and using time and resources in an efficient manner.
2. To provide guidance for modifying or explicating the programmes' action plan as needed, particularly since not all aspects of the plan can be anticipated or planned in advance.
3. To assess periodically the extent to which programmes' personnel are performing their rules and charting out their responsibilities.
4. To provide an extension record of the programmes, how it was implemented and how it compares to what was intended.

7.3 IPO (Input, Process, and Output) Model of Training Evaluation

Combining and enhancing features of both Kirkpatrick's four level models and Brinkerhoff's six-stage model, IBM developed its own model for training evaluation. Bushnell (1990) developed the IPO model (input, process, and output) which focuses more on the inputs to training with a view to improve corporate education strategy. In the early stage of evaluation, it takes into account some of the factors (input) that may affect training's effectiveness. Among these factors are trainee qualifications, trainer qualifications, program design, materials, facilities and equipment. The inputs, themselves subject to evaluation, are fed into the process stage where the mechanics of planning, designing, developing and delivering the training are accomplished. After the delivery of training, the results are evaluated. The stages of IPO are as follows:

1. Inputs—instructor experience, trainee qualifications, resources.
2. Process—plan, design, development and delivery of training.

3. Outputs—trainees' reactions, knowledge and skills gained and improved job performance.
4. Outcomes—profits, customer satisfaction and productivity.

7.4 TVS (Training Valuation System)

Fitz-enz (1994) developed a Training Valuation System (TVS) which is a four step process similar to Kirkpatrick's framework at steps 3 and 4 but has been categorized as "system-based". The steps involved include:

1. **Step 1:** Situation—analysis is similar to an in-depth training analysis. Like Kearns and Miller, he suggested that the manager's answers are continuously probed until some visible, tangible outcome is revealed and that the questions initially focus on the work process rather than the training;
2. **Step 2:** Intervention—this involves diagnosing the problem and designing the training;
3. **Step 3:** Impact—this examines the variables that impact performance.
4. **Step 4:** Value—this step places a monetary worth on the changed performance.

7.5 Guskey's Critical Levels

Thomas Guskey (2002) also explained/redefined Kirkpatrick's 4 levels into 5. These five levels of the model may be of significance as he had taken "students" and educational environment into consideration:

Level 1: Participant Reaction:

- **Objective:** To measure the participants' reactions about information and basic human needs.
- **Technique:** Generally a questionnaire.
- **Main Questions:** Was your time well spent? Was the presenter knowledgeable? Information give to you was fruitful or not?

Level 2: Participant learning

- **Objective:** To examine participants' level of achieved learning.

- **Technique:** Test, simulation, personal reflection, full-scale demonstration.
- **Key Question:** Did participants learn what was planned?

Level 3: Organizational Support and Learning

- **Purpose:** To examine organizational support for skills gained in staff development.
- **Technique:** Minutes of district meetings, questionnaires, structured interviews or unremarkable observations.
- **Main Questions:** Were problems addressed rapidly and competently? Were adequate funds made available, including time for reflection?

Level 4: Participant Use of New Knowledge and Skills

- **Objective:** To determine whether participants are using what they learned and using it well.
- **Technique:** Questionnaires, structured interviews, oral or written personal reflections, examination of journals or portfolio, or direct observation.
- **Key Question:** Are participants implementing their skills and to what degree?

Level 5: Student Learning Outcomes

- **Objective:** To analyze the correlating student learning objectives.
- **Technique:** Classroom grades, tests, direct observation.
- **Main Question:** Did students show improvement in academic, behaviour or other parts?

7.6 Jack Philip's ROI Method

Jack Phillips is an internationally renowned expert on measuring the return on investment (ROI) of human resource development activities. In his many books and articles, Phillips has gone beyond even Kirkpatrick's level 4 to focus on real measurement of ROI (justification of the cost of training based on the return on investment and organizational impact). ROI has become increasingly important to investors in training programs as global competition has increased and fiscal belts have tightened. This method observes the gain from training intervention and is then compared to the per person cost of training to decide whether or not a particular training or evaluation should be continued.

This approach not only enables an organization to calculate the financial ROI from the training event, but also helps decide whether changes need to be made in evaluation techniques or in training, and thus it can be useful during formative evaluation. The ROI can also indicate if the evaluation is "worth" the investment. Jack Philip's ROI model includes following levels:

1. **Reaction, Satisfaction and Planned Action:** Measures the extent to which the participants enjoyed the learning experience and establishes how they plan to apply their learning.
2. **Learning:** Measures the extent to which the participants have increased their knowledge and improved their skill levels.
3. **Application and Implementation:** Measures the extent to which the participants have applied to their working practice, what they learnt from the learning event.
4. **Business Impact:** Measures the results that the participants have achieved as a result of applying what they learnt from the learning event. This would include measures such as output, quality, cost, time, customer satisfaction and employee satisfaction.
5. **Return on Investment:** Measures the level of monetary benefit and the overall cost of the learning event and then compares the two. Usually expressed as a percentage of cost-benefit ratio.

7.7 CIRO Model of Evaluation

This model was developed in 1970 by Warr, Bird and Rackham. CIRO remains one of the most widely used training evaluation models. Although over 30 years old, it strikes a chord with some of the key issues that trainers are still grappling with today: how to demonstrate the impact of training on organizational objectives, and, in turn, how to make a strong business case for training. This model demonstrates that the training department, like all other departments, will be expected to play its part in the achievement of the organization's objectives. If trainers can demonstrate factually that they are making a genuine contribution to the organization's goals, this can lead to an increase in both the standing and influence of the training department within that organization. The amount of support given by other members of the organization will rest largely on the regard they have for the training department staff. So any activity which heightens that regard will ultimately benefit from the training function.

The model is based on four stages or types of evaluation—context, input, reactions and outcome—and is underpinned by a set of three questions, which, according to the authors, the trainer should always bear in mind:

1. What needs to be changed?
2. What procedures are most likely to bring about this change?
3. What evidence is there that change has occurred?

7.8 Cost-benefit Analysis

Cost-benefit analysis (CBA) is an evaluation method used to determine the economic benefits of a training program using accounting methods, which comprise of training cost and benefits. When training is imparted to the employees, afterwards, cost-benefit analysis is established to determine whether there was any training benefit associated with the training costs. It is a very popular approach to calculate return on investment (ROI). It is used in both planning and evaluation of a training program. In planning, it helps to predict whether the benefits of training will be equal to or greater than the costs of the training. In evaluation, it is like a measurement of how well training as a solution fits the problem for which it was planned. This provides a framework for analyzing data in a logical and consistent way. Cost-benefit analysis (CBA) helps an organization answer questions such as:

1. Does the training program provide a net benefit to the organization as a whole?
2. Should the proposed training project, programme or policy be

undertaken?

3. Should the training project or programme be sustained?
4. Which of various alternative training projects or programmcs should be undertaken?

Different approaches to evaluation of training discussed herein indicate that the activities involved in evaluation of training are complex and not always well-structured. Since evaluation activities in training situations involve multiple goals associated with multiple levels, evaluation should perhaps be viewed as a collaborative activity between training designers, training managers, trainers, floor managers, and possibly others.

Short Answer Type Questions

1. Discuss the various models of training evaluation.
2. How are the models of training essential for an organization?
3. What is cost-benefit analysis?
4. What is reaction CIRO model of training evaluation?

Long Answer Type Questions

1. Illustrate with examples the merits and demerits of models of training evaluation available for measuring the effectiveness of training.
2. How CBA is helpful in calculating ROI?

Multiple Choice Questions

Q. 1. Expense of training, materials of training, salary and time of trainees and trainers are classified as

a. Typical costs
b. Typical benefits
c. Post-measure variables
d. Pre-measures variables

Q. 2. While describing the individual roles, the 'role' is termed as

a. Individual role
b. Focal role
c. Social role

d. none of the above

Q. 3. Improving current and future management performance is called

a. Management development
b. Job rotation
c. Job training
d. Lifelong learning

Q. 4. Method in which teams consisting of managers compete on solving problems is called

a. Management game
b. Action learning
c. Lifelong learning
d. Case study method

Q. 5. A technique involving trainees to act on role of specific person in real situation is called

a. Behaviour modelling
b. Role playing
c. In-house development centre
d. Both a and b

Q. 6. Technique in which trainees are shown films on management techniques is called

a. Behaviour modelling
b. Role playing
c. In-house development centre
d. Both a and b

Q. 7. _______is widely used for human relations and leadership training

a. Business games
b. Role playing
c. Case study method
d. Job rotation

Q. 8. The type of training which is used as a tool for developing interpersonal, decision-making and analytical skills within the trainee is called

a. Case study
b. Sensitivity training
c. On the job training
d. Equipment simulators

Q. 9. What is the process of training and developing employees to improve and update their knowledge and skills so as to perform their jobs better known as?

a. Human resource development
b. Employment
c. Compensation management
d. Managing employee relations

Q. 10. Which amongst the following factors are considered to analyze a person's behaviour in Expectancy Theory?

a. Valence
b. Instrumentality
c. Expectancy
d. All of these

Q. 11. One of the important principles of a Project Method is

a. The Principle of Structure
b. The Principle of Generality
c. The Principle of Activity
d. The Principle of Assumption
e.

Q. 12. Which of the following is not a type of Project?

a. The dill type
b. The problem type
c. The producer type
d. The supplier type

Q. 13. Action learning is a

a. Creative problem solving method
b. Education based method
c. Sabbatical method
d. University related method

Q. 14. Which of the following is not an element of Action Learning Method
a. Problem
b. Inflection
c. Set
d. Set advisor

Q. 15. What is called as a training in which trainees share their innermost feelings openly with the group in the presence of a trained facilitator or psychologist?
a. Workshop
b. Conference
c. Sensitivity
d. Role play

Q. 16. Sensitivity training is also known by the name of
a. National training
b. "Here and How" training
c. "There and Then" training
d. T-group training

Q. 17. One possible problem in sensitivity training is
a. Lack of experienced trainers
b. De-motivating group behaviour
c. Punished by organizations
d. Lack of team training

Q. 18. Formative evaluation is
a. Paused monitoring of the training effectiveness
b. Continuous monitoring of the training effectiveness to facilitate onward correction and modification

c. Obtain feedback on the effectiveness of training programme
d. A defined duration of effectiveness of training programme

Q. 19. Which of the following is not a principle of evaluation
a. Objectivity
b. Feedback
c. Reliability
d. Clarity

Answer Key

Q.1.	C	Q.11.	C
Q.2.	B	Q.12.	D
Q.3.	A	Q.13.	A
Q.4.	A	Q.14.	B
Q.5.	B	Q.15.	C
Q.6.	A	Q.16.	D
Q.7.	B	Q.17.	C
Q.8.	A	Q.18	B
Q.9.	A	Q.19	B
Q.10.	D		

8

Organizational Development: Definitions and Characteristics

Organizational (or organization) development or simply OD. is a technique of planned change. It seeks to change beliefs, attitudes, values and structures—in fact the entire culture of the organization—so that an organization may better adapt to technology and live with the pace of change. OD is a comprehensive strategy for organization improvement. OD is a long range effort to improve an organization's problem solving and renewal processes, particularly through a more effective and collaborative management culture.

Organizational development is a field of research, theory, and practice dedicated to expanding the knowledge and effectiveness of people to accomplish more successful organizational changes and performances. It is a process of continuous diagnosis, action planning, implementation and evaluation, with the goal of transferring knowledge and skills to organizations to improve their capacity for solving problems and managing future change.

8.1 Definitions of the Concept

A few definitions of organizational development as under:

According to Koonzei, "OD is a systematic integrated and planned approach to improve the effectiveness of an enterprise. It is designed to solve problems that adversely affect the operational efficiency at all levels".

Burke' has defined OD as "a planned process of change in an organization's culture through the utilization of behavioural science, technology, research and theory".

Schmuck and Miles, defined OD as "a planned and sustained effort to apply behavioural science for system improvement, using reflexive, self-analytic methods".

8.2 Origins and History of OD

The history of OD has been developed with valuable contributions of very renowned behavioural researchers and experts. The history of OD can be essentially divided into 4 parts:

1. Survey research and feedback methodology.
2. Innovations in applying laboratory training insights to complex organizations.
3. The above two parts are intertwined with a third, the occurrence of action research.
4. Paralleling to the above three, and to some extent linked, the fourth one is the emergence of the Travistock socio-technical and social-clinical approach.

The key actors in these areas interact with each other and are influenced by experiences and concepts from many fields.

8.3 Characteristics of OD

The salient characteristics of OD implied in its definitions are gleaned as follows:

1. Organizational development is an educational strategy for bringing a planned change.
2. It is related to real problems of the organization.
3. Laboratory training methods based on experienced behaviour are primarily used to bring change.
4. OD uses change agent (or consultant) to guide and affect change. The role of change agent is to guide groups towards more effective group processes rather than telling them what to do. Change agents simply assist the group in problem solving processes and the groups solve the problems themselves.
5. There is a close working relationship between change agents and the people who are being changed.
6. OD seeks to build problem-solving capacity by improving group dynamics and problem confrontation.
7. OD reaches into all aspects of the organization culture in order to make it more humanly responsive.
8. OD is a long-term approach (of 3 to 5 years period) and is

meant to elevate the organization to a higher level of functioning by improving the performance and satisfaction of the organization members.

9. OD is broad-based and describes a variety of change programmes. It is concerned not only with changes in organizational design but also with changes in organizational philosophies, skills of individuals and groups.
10. OD is a dynamic process. It recognizes that the goals of an organization change and hence the methods of attaining them should also change.
11. OD utilizes systems thinking. It is based on an open, adaptive systems concept. The organization is treated as an interrelated whole and no part of the organization can be changed without affecting the other parts.
12. OD is research based. Change agents conduct surveys, collect data, evaluate and then decisions are taken.
13. OD uses group processes rather than individual process. It makes efforts to improve group performance.
14. OD is situational and contingency-oriented.
15. Organization development and management development are complementary rather than conflicting.

8.4 Objectives of OD

The main objectives of OD are as follows:

1. Improve organizational performance as measured by profitability, market share, innovativeness, etc.
2. Make organizations better adaptive to its environment which always keeps on changing.
3. Make the members willing to face organizational problems and contribute creative solutions to organizational problems.
4. Improve internal behaviour patterns such as interpersonal relations, inter-group relations, level of trust and support among the role players.
5. Understand openness and meaningful communication and involvement in planning for organizational development.

8.5 Basic Components of OD

OD has three basic components, listed below:

1. **Diagnosis:** It represents a continuous collection of date about the total system, its subunits, its processes, and its culture.
2. **Action:** It consists of all the activities and interventions designed to improve an organization's functioning.
3. **Programme Management:** It encompasses all activities designed to ensure success of the program.

8.6 Process of Organization Development

OD process comprises of three basic components viz. diagnosis, action and program management. Diagnostic component is about continuous collection of data about the total system, its sub-units, its process and its culture. The action component represents all the actions and interventions that are designed to increase organizational effectiveness. The programme management component consists of all the activities designed to ensure success of the OD process.

8.6.1 Diagnosis: The first step is to diagnose the current system of an organization's or client's system. It involves the client system's concerns, unrealized opportunities, discrepancies or gap between actual and desired performance. Diagnosis starts with data collection about the system its sub-units and processes. Diagnostic activities provide the real picture of a client system. Diagnosis can be done by designing questionnaires, observations or conducting interviews and meetings. Diagnosis is a continuous process which is necessary for planned change effort.

8.6.2 Action Component: OD interventions are sets of structural activities in which selected organizational units are engaged in sequence of tasks for organizational improvement. Interventions are actions taken to produce the desired changes. Planning actions, implementing them and evaluating the consequences of actions are distinguishing features of OD.

8.6.3 Programme Management: Managing OD program effectively is crucial issue. It follows sequence of activities such as:

1. **Entering into an OD Relationship:** The OD program starts with a contract of a client system with OD consultant. This step starts with addressing and clarifying the issue or a problem. The client system and the OD consultant discuss the problem and collect the data for further process. Client system must know the expertise and competence of OD consultant and client must also be able to present the problem or issue clearly.
2. **Contracting:** OD contract is about expectations of both the parties. OD contract helps to develop a commitment and support which is required for the entire process.
3. **Diagnosis:** Diagnosis of an organization helps the consultant to find out current functioning of an organization. It is basically a fact finding activity. Diagnosis is a collaborative effort. Both organizational members and consultant should be involved in discovering the current organizational effectiveness.
4. **Feedback:** It represents feeding back the information gained through diagnosis for analysis of the client along with consultant thereby exploring the information which gives a clear picture of the current situation.
5. **Planning Change:** The feedback which is received leads to plan the change efforts required and opportunities can be discussed for further action steps.
6. **Intervention:** After deciding action steps, it becomes necessary to think on various activities to implement planned change efforts. These activities are sets of actions designed to correct or improve the problem situation or even to seize the opportunities. These are called as OD interventions.
7. **Evaluation:** This step represents analysis of the implementation of various activities as a part of the OD program. If successful, reasons for success, various changes or modifications occurring during the process and satisfaction with the results are some of the parameters of evaluation.

8.7 F)undations of OD

OD follows certain foundations or also called as core values that help OD practitioner to design appropriate OD interventions. These foundations act as guidelines for an effective OD program.

8.7.1 Planned Change: Change means the new state of things is different from old state of things. Change is everywhere; change will be one of the few constants during the end of this century and into the next. Change has different facets, for example, it can be deliberate or accidental. Its magnitude can be large or small. It can affect many elements of an organization or only a few. It can be fast or slow. The new state of things can have an entirely different nature from the old state of things or new state of things can have the same nature modifications.

The models for planned change are as follows:

1. **Motivating Change:** The first step is getting people want to change, to believe change is necessary and to commit to abandoning the status quo for an uncertain future. There are three methods for creating readiness to change. One of the greatest motivator for change is that things aren't working to generate profits and market share is dropping, and consequently, survival is in doubt. These conditions increase readiness for change. One of the oldest and most effective strategies for overcoming resistance is to involve organizational members directly in planning and implementation change.
2. **Creating a Vision:** It provides a picture of the future and show how individuals and groups fit into that future. Well defined vision reduces uncertainty and serves as a goal to energize behaviour, show that the future will be beneficial, and demonstrate that future is attainable.
3. **Developing Political Support:** It is critical in successful change efforts. Powerful individuals and groups must be convinced that change is good for them or at least will not significantly harm them.
4. **Managing the Transition:** It means managing complex change. Beckhard and Harris propose that change effort

moves through three states, namely, the current state, the transition state, and the desired state, and suggest three set of activities for managing the transition state including activity planning, commitment planning, and management structures.

8.7.2 Kurt Lewin's Process of Change: Kurt Lewin introduced to ideas about change that have been influential since 1940. The first idea states that what is occurring at any point of time is a resultant in a field of opposing force. That is the status quo—whatever is happening right now is the result of focus pushing in opposing direction. For example, we can think of the production level of a manufacturing plant as a resultant equilibrium point in a field of force, with some focus pushing towards a higher level of production and some focus pushing towards a lower level of production. Lewin's second idea was a model of change process itself. He suggested that change is a three stage process—unfreezing the old behaviour, moving to a new level of behaviour and refreezing the behaviour at the new level. Change entails moving from one equilibrium point to another. Lewin's description of the process of change involves three steps. Figure 8.1 summarizes the steps and processes involved in a planned change through action research. Action research is depicted as a cyclical process of change.

1. The cycle begins with a series of planning actions initiated by the client and the change agent working together. The principal elements of this stage include a preliminary diagnosis, data gathering, feedback of results, and joint action planning. In the language of systems theory, this is the input phase, in which a client system becomes aware of the problems as yet unidentified, realizes it may need outside help to effect changes, and shares with the consultant the process of problem diagnosis.
2. The second stage of action research is the action, or transformation phase. This stage includes actions relating to learning processes (perhaps in the form of role analysis) and to planning and executing behavioural changes in the client organization. As shown in Figure 8.1, feedback at this stage

would move via feedback loop A and would have the effect of altering previous planning to bring the learning activities of the client system into better alignment with change objectives. Included in this stage is action-planning activity carried out jointly by the consultant and members of the client system. Following the workshop or learning sessions, these action steps are carried out on the job as part of the transformation stage.

Figure 8.1: Steps and Processes Involved in a Planned Change

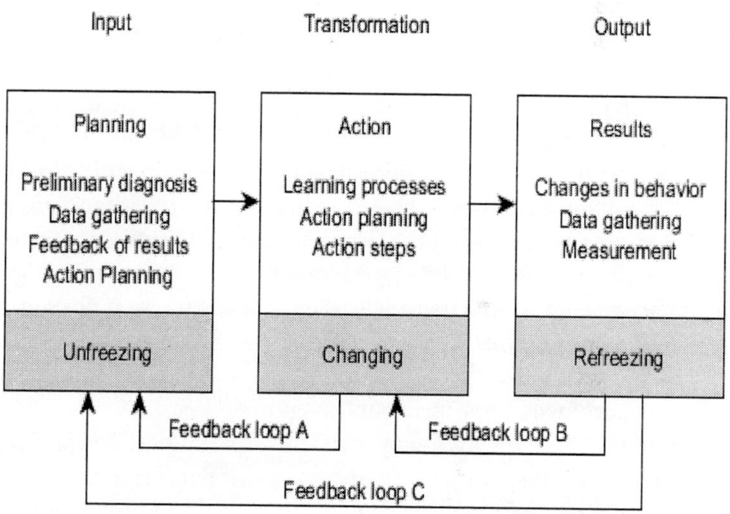

3. The third stage of action research is the output or results phase. This stage includes actual changes in behaviour (if any) resulting from corrective action steps taken following the second stage. Data is again gathered from the client system so that progress can be determined and necessary adjustments in learning activities can be made. Minor adjustments of this nature can be made in learning activities via feedback loop B.

8.8 OD Action Research Process

Action research is a process which serves as a model for most OD interventions. French and Bell (1995) describe action research as a "process of systematically collecting research data about an ongoing system relative to some objective, goal, or need of that system; feeding this data back into the system; taking actions by altering selected variables within the system based both on the data and on hypotheses; and evaluating the results of actions by collecting more data".

The steps in action research are as under:

1. **Entry:** This phase consists of finding needs for change within an organization. It is also the time to quickly grasp the nature of the organization, identify the appropriate decision-maker, and build a trusting relationship.
2. **Start-up and Contracting:** In this step, critical success factors and real issues are identified. We link into the organization's culture and processes, and clarify roles for the consultant(s) and employees. This is also the time to deal with resistance within the organization. A formal or informal contract will define the change process.
3. **Assessment and Diagnosis:** Here, the data is collected to find opportunities and problems in an organization. This is also the time for the consultant to make a diagnosis, in order to recommend appropriate interventions.
4. **Feedback:** This two-way process serves to tell what was found out, based on an analysis of the data. Everyone who contributed information should have an opportunity to learn about the findings of the assessment process (provided there is no apparent breach of anyone's confidentiality.) The feedback should start with the executive client and his/her team. Usuaily, it is cascaded down through the organization to reach all who have participated. This provides an opportunity for the organization's people to become involved in the change process, to learn about how different parts of the organization affect each other, and to participate in selecting appropriate change interventions.

5. **Planning Change:** In this step, recommendations are distilled from the assessment and feedback. Alternative actions are considered and the focus of the intervention(s) is on activities that have the most leverage to effect positive change in an organization. An implementation plan is developed that is based on the assessment data, is logically organized, result-oriented, measurable and rewarded. The next step is to plan for a participative decision-making process for the intervention.
6. **Intervention:** Now, and only now, the actual change process is carried out. It is important to follow the action plan, yet remain flexible enough to modify the process as the organization changes and as new information emerges.
7. **Evaluation:** Successful OD must have made meaningful changes in the performance and efficiency of the people and their organization. An evaluation procedure to verify this success, identify needs for new or continuing OD activities, and improve the OD process itself to help make future interventions more successful is needed.
8. **Adoption:** After steps have been made to change an organization and plans have been formulated, follow-up is started by implementing processes to insure that this remains an ongoing activity within the organization, that commitments for action have been obtained, and that they will be carried out.
9. **Separation:** It must recognize when it is more productive for the client and consultant to undertake other activities, and when continued consultation is counterproductive. The change should be monitored for its success possibly to plan for future change activities.

8.8.1 Significance of Action Research:

1. The identification of a problem area about which an individual or a group is sufficiently concerned to want to take some action.
2. The selection of a specific problem and the formulation of a hypothesis or prediction that implies a goal and a procedure

reaching it.

3. The careful recording of an action taken and the accumulation of evidence to determine the degree to which the goal has been achieved.
4. The interference from this evidence of generalization regarding the relation between the action and the desired goal.
5. The continuous retesting of this generalization in action situations.

But for successful OD to take place, all of these steps must be followed. It works best if they are taken in the order described. And, since learning is really an iterative, not a sequential process, one must be prepared to re-enter this process when and where appropriate.

1. **Systems Theory:** According to this theory, organizations are viewed as open systems which can actively exchange with their environment. Open system involves inputs, throughputs and outputs. Inputs are from environment like energy, information, money, people etc. Throughput is conversion or transformation of inputs into outputs. System is delineated by a boundary into internal system and external environment. The boundary of open system permits exchange with internal processes and external environment.
2. **Applied Behavioural Science:** OD is based on applied behavioural science. Human resources are affected by change and if change needs to be successful it has to consider human side of it. So, OD interventions are designed based on applied behavioural science.
3. **Participation and Empowerment:** This is a unique feature of OD and also an important foundation. It is not restricted to top level of an organization but also throughout the organization. To empower is to give someone power to take decisions. Employees are empowered in OD by giving them authority in OD programs. Participation in some or the other way enhances empowerment. Many of the OD interventions are deliberately designed to increase involvement and

participation.

4. **Teams and Team Work:** Team plays a major role in organizational success. Complex tasks can be performed in a better way through teamwork. Teams play a crucial role in change efforts. Team building interventions are specially designed interventions to increase team performance.
5. **Normative Re-educative Strategy:** It is based on the assumptions that norms form the basis of the behaviour and change comes through re-education in which old norms are discarded and supplemented with new ones.

Points to Remember

1. OD is a systematic integrated and planned approach to improve the effectiveness of the enterprise. It is designed to solve problems that adversely affect operational efficiency at all levels.
2. OD uses change agent (or consultant) to guide and affect the change. The role of a change agent is to guide groups towards more effective group processes rather than telling them what to do. Change agents simply assist the groups in problem solving processes and the groups solve the problems themselves.
3. It is concerned not only with changes in organizational design but also with changes in organizational philosophies, skills of individuals and groups.
4. OD process comprises of three basic components—diagnosis, action and program management.
5. Action research is a process which serves as a model for most OD interventions.

Short Answer Type Questions

1. Define organizational development.
2. Who are change agents?
3. Is OD a long-term or a short-term approach?
4. Explain Kurt Lewin's process of change.
5. What is a system theory?

6. OD mainly has three basic components. What are those components?
7. Define planned change? Why is it important for the survival for an organization?

Long Answer Type Questions

1. Why organizational development is important in an organization? Discuss the process of OD in detail.
2. Discuss the origin of organizational development.
3. How foundation of organizational development is helpful for an organization?
4. What is an action research? Discuss the process of action research.
5. Discuss the various characteristics of organizational development.

Multiple Choice Questions

Q. 1. In Lewin's organization change process, introduction of new attitudes and behaviour is included in

a. Unfreezing stage
b. Moving stage
c. Refreezing stage
d. Non-moving stage

Q. 2. OD process is cyclical and ends when

a. Desired development results are obtained
b. Plan is implemented
c. Data is gathered
d. Problem is identified

Q. 3. Role negotiation technique for group intervention was developed by

a. Roger Harrison
b. Bennet and Hailey
c. Both a and b
d. None of the above

Q. 4. OD can also be called as a process

a. For performance appraisal
b. For change of people
c. For teaching people how to solve the problem
d. All of the above

Q. 5. OD intervention seminars being conducted in the organization help to

a. Improve overall efficiency
b. Improve productivity
c. Improve overall morale of the employees
d. All of the above

Q. 6. Cultural intervention concentrates on

a. Traditions
b. Precedents
c. Practices
d. All of the above

Q. 7. During the course of the organisational development projects, the internal OD specialists should

a. Become increasingly professionalized and be responsible for their own development
b. Advise the consultant
c. Both a and b
d. None of the above

Q. 8. One of the major purposes of action research is

a. Re-searching on an action
b. Perform environmental analysis
c. Designing better training programs
d. Build a body of scientific knowledge around that action

Q. 9. Unfreezing refers to

a. Diagnosing situation
b. Becoming aware of a need to change

c. Exploring new models of change
d. Reinforcing new behaviour

Q. 10. OD interventions are basically
a. Action on a previous research
b. Skill-based outcomes
c. Principal learning process in action
d. Personal improvement

Answer Key

Q.1.	B	Q.6.	D
Q.2.	A	Q.7.	A
Q.3.	A	Q.8.	D
Q.4.	D	Q.9.	B
Q.5.	D	Q.10.	C

9

Organizational Development Interventions

Organizational development (OD) intervention refers to the set of structured activities in which selected organizational units (target groups or individuals) engage with a task or a sequence of tasks where the task goals are related directly or indirectly to organizational improvement. OD interventions basically help organizations in problem solving and renewal. OD offers a variety of interventions based on the problem. Designing and implementation of appropriate OD interventions help to achieve the desired goals.

9.1 Definitions of OD Interventions

According to Cummings and Worley, "OD intervention is a sequence of activities, actions and events intended to help organizations improve their performance and effectiveness".

According to French and Bell, "Organizational development interventions are sets of structured activities in which selected organizational units (target groups or individuals) engage with a task or a sequence of tasks where the task goals are related directly or indirectly to organizational improvement. Interventions constitute the action thrust of organization development; they make things happen and are what is happening". Several techniques have been included under the OD programme.

9.2 Evolution of OD Interventions

The roots of evolution of OD interventions can go deep in scientific management as they are aimed at change for increased productivity of an organization. The human relation movement incorporated the human side in the process of enhancing organizational performance. The process of evolution of OD intervention was a landmark following its invention by Kurt Lewin and his theory of planned change. This theory stated that if change is managed with planned efforts it can be successful. So, for planned change efforts, various behavioural scientists proposed OD interventions. The contributions from these scientists have helped an organization to understand the entire process of change in a systematic way. The term organization development was later formed as there was a need to have specialized efforts for effective change management. This assignment of the term helped to combine all the efforts under one umbrella.

The evolution of OD interventions thus comprise of a laboratory stem, survey feedback stem, action research stem and socio-technical stem. The process is still going on with extensive research done by various OD practitioners and researchers. The field of OD interventions is increasing day-by-day and helps an organization to sustain in this era of continuous change. The evolution of OD and OD interventions is shaped by various experiments and contributions by founders in the field. The milestones in the evolution of OD and OD interventions can be elaborated as follows:

1. The human relation movement introduced the concept of unleashing human potential through various OD interventions.
2. Founders like Kurt Lewin initiated the idea of theoretical roots to various OD interventions and theories in OD. The work of Ron Lippit at NTL also introduced interventions related to group development.
3. Interventions like T-groups and socio-technical systems (STS) were introduced by Tavistock Institute in UK.
4. The development of survey research methods derived and designed by Likert and Mann emphasized the need for collection of data and evolution of survey research OD interventions.
5. The action research and diagnostic interventions proved to be very important as it gave rise to interventions for accurate

diagnosis and effective organizational change management.

6. The evolution of Japanese management techniques also proved essential as system wide interventions for organizational effectiveness.
7. OD interventions like learning organizations by Peter Senge or grid concept by Blake and Mouton proved to be beneficial for the organizations in a competitive era.
8. The evolution still continues with recent interventions like appreciative enquiry which is also one of the most powerful interventions.

9.3 Features of OD Interventions

1. OD interventions are planned activities.
2. OD interventions refer to implementation of entire OD program systematically.
3. OD interventions are decided mutually by client and a consultant.
4. Selection of appropriate OD intervention denotes careful diagnosis of current system of an organization.
5. Application of OD interventions requires participation and involvement of a client system.
6. OD interventions focus on social and task performance enhancement.
7. OD interventions differ from organization to organization based on requirement.
8. Success of OD intervention depends on the knowledge and expertise of an OD consultant, either internal or external.

9.4 Types of OD Interventions

1. **Diagnostic Activities:** These are fact finding activities designed to find the current state of a client system.
2. **Team Building Activities:** These are designed to enhance effective operation of teams.
3. **Inter-group Activities:** These are the activities designed to improve effectiveness of interdependent groups.
4. **Survey Feedback Activities:** These activities rely on

gathering information that is used in understanding problems or opportunities.

5. **Education and Training Activities:** These are activities designed to improve an individual's skills, abilities and knowledge.
6. **Techno Structural or Structural Activities:** These activities are designed to improve the effectiveness of organizational structure and job design.
7. **Process Consultation Activities:** These activities are designed in consultation with a client to perceive, understand and act upon events that occur in a client's environment.
8. **Grid Organization Development Activities:** These activities were developed by Robert Blake and Mouton which consist of a six phase model involving the whole organization.
9. **Third Party Peacemaking Activities:** These activities are designed and conducted by skilled consultants to manage inter-personal conflict in the process of organizational change.
10. **Coaching and Counselling Activities:** These activities help individuals to define learning goals, to understand the behaviour of others and see how others watch their behaviour.
11. **Life and Career Planning Activities:** These activities enable individuals to focus on their life and career objectives and ways to achieve them.
12. **Planning and Goal Setting Activities:** These activities include goal setting, problem solving, and discrepancies if any to achieve the objectives.
13. **Strategic Management Activities:** These activities link interventions with basic mission and environmental scanning which helps in long-term planning.
14. **Organization Transformation activities:** These activities involve large scale system changes or fundamental changes in the nature of an organization.

Each of the above mentioned interventions include many

activities. Some of the activities are problem specific and some are process specific.

9.5 Benefits of OD Interventions

1. OD interventions are range of tools and techniques used to managed change effectively. An organization can select appropriate OD intervention as per the needs.
2. OD interventions are based on OD values and assumptions which focus on behavioural, technical and structural aspects of change.
3. OD interventions promote individual well-being and enhanced performance.
4. Team building interventions create team effectiveness for organizational effectiveness. The conflict is effectively resolved through inter-group or confrontation OD interventions.
5. OD interventions not only help in understanding the job requirements but also the role and responsibility in the process.
6. Effective implementation of OD interventions creates a responsive and adaptive culture in an organization.
7. The range of OD interventions offers large scale transformational tools and techniques for sustainability of an organization.
8. OD interventions involve empowerment of employees.
9. The process of implementation of OD interventions helps in selecting appropriate OD intervention for shared vision, motivating change, enhanced performance and organizational effectiveness.

9.6 Problems Faced in Implementation of OD Interventions

1. The objectives of change if not clear and communicated to the change targets can lead to misinterpretation of OD efforts.
2. Lack of trust and support from top management can also be a hurdle in the implementation of OD interventions.
3. The expertise of OD consultant, either internal or external, is

crucial in the entire process of implementation of OD interventions.

4. The selection of appropriate OD intervention is also important, if it is not done through proper diagnosis and research, can lead to the failure of entire process.
5. The change targets need clear vision and communication for the entire process of implementation of OD process; lack of this can give rise to resistance to change.
6. Resistance to change is one of the critical aspects in the implementation process of OD interventions.
7. The feedback loop if missing in the entire process can mislead the real objectives of OD process.
8. The implementation of OD interventions cannot be considered as quick fix but they need continuous updation as per the changing demands.
9. Lack of proper evaluation techniques can also be a critical issue in the implementation of OD interventions.
10. OD intervention cannot be implemented in parts but it needs a holistic approach.

9.7 Parameters for Ideal OD Interventions

1. Application of OD intervention needs a systematic approach.
2. OD intervention should be applied based on the need or problem of an organization.
3. Application of OD intervention is different for different organizations.
4. Implementation of OD intervention needs expertise of internal or external consultants.
5. The process of application of OD interventions is continuous.
6. Employees must be well aware of application of OD interventions and should know the motive behind implementation of a particular OD intervention.
7. The entire process of implementation should follow the values and assumptions of OD, i.e. action research, survey feedback, teams and team work, parallel learning structure, normative and re-educative strategy, open systems,

involvement and participation etc.

8. Evaluation of OD interventions should be done systematically.
9. Application of behaviour science in designing and implementation of OD intervention enhances effectiveness.
10. Selection of appropriate OD intervention needs careful diagnosis which enhances the success of application of OD interventions.

9.8 Role of HR in Implementation of OD Interventions for Managing Change

HR department is responsible for developing the most important asset of an organization and good HR practice delivers organizational performance that achieves organizational objectives successfully. HR aims to develop manpower according to objectives and goals of an organization. Therefore, when an organization faces challenges to sustain, it is the responsibility of HR department to prepare employees for the upcoming challenges.

Following are the areas of concern in implementation of OD interventions program in managing organizational change:

1. Creating awareness for change.
2. Motivating employees for change.
3. Explaining needs for change to employees.

Points to Remember

1. OD intervention is a sequence of activities actions and events intended to help an organization improve its performance and effectiveness.
2. OD offers variety of interventions based on the problem.
3. The roots of evolution of OD interventions can go deep in scientific management as it also aimed at change for increased productivity of an organization. The process of evolution of OD intervention was a landmark following the invention by Kurt Lewin and his theory of planned change.
4. OD interventions are planned activities and the success of

OD intervention depends on the knowledge and expertise of an OD consultants, either internal or external.

5. OD interventions are range of tools and techniques used to manage change effectively. An organization can select appropriate OD interventions as per the needs and these are based on OD values and assumptions which focus on behavioural, technical and structural aspects of change.

Short Answer Type questions

1. Define OD intervention.
2. What do you mean by team building activities?
3. What are the main purposes of life and career planning activities?
4. Who was the main contributor in the emergence of OD interventions?
5. Why action research and diagnostic interventions proved to be important for OD interventions?

Long Answer Type Questions

1. Elaborate the evolution of OD interventions.
2. Define organizational development. What are the various features of OD interventions?
3. Discuss the various types of OD interventions in detail.
4. What are the benefits of OD interventions? Why organizations believe OD interventions are important for their survival?
5. Why is the role of a HR manager important in implementing OD interventions?
6. Discuss the parameters of ideal OD interventions.

10

Team Interventions

Twenty five years ago, when companies like W.L. Gore, Volvo, and General Foods introduced teams into their production processes, it made news because no one else was doing it. Today, it is just the opposite. It is the organization that does not use teams that has become newsworthy. Currently, 80 percent of Fortune 500 companies have half or more of their employees on teams. 68 percent of small U.S manufacturers are using teams in their production areas. The evidence suggests that teams typically outperform individuals when the tasks being done require multiple skills, judgment, and experience. As organizations have restructured themselves to compete more effectively and efficiently, they have turned to teams as a way to use employee talent in a better fashion. Management has found that teams are more flexible and responsive to changing events than are traditional departments or other forms of permanent grouping. Teams have the capability to quickly assemble, deploy, refocus, and disband. Collaborative management of the work team culture is a fundamental emphasis of organization development programmes.

It is important to make a distinction between a 'work group' and a 'work team'. *A work group* is a group that interacts primarily to share information and to make decisions to help each group member perform within his or her area of responsibility. There is no positive synergy that would create an overall level of performance that is greater than the sum of the inputs. In a work group, members usually report to a common superior and have some face-to-face interaction, who have some degree of interdependence in carrying out tasks for the purpose of achieving organizational goals. *A work team* is a group whose individual efforts result in a performance that is greater than the sum of individual inputs. It generates positive synergy through coordinated efforts. Work team has some characteristics in greater degree than ordinary groups, including a higher commitment to common goals and a higher degree of interdependency and interaction. According to Jon Katzenbach and Douglas Smith, 'a team is a small number of people with complementary skills who are committed to a common purpose, set of performance goals, and approach for which they hold themselves mutually accountable'.

10.1 Types of Teams

There are various kinds of teams that are helpful in organizational development. These are as follows:

10.1.1 Cross-Functional Teams: These types of teams are widely used in organizations, and have great utility in the formation and ongoing functioning of these teams. These teams are typically comprised of individuals who are of same hierarchical level, but from different work areas, who meet regularly to solve ongoing challenges requiring input from a number of functional areas. Such teams might be permanent, but temporary teams can be created to solve short-term problems such as planning a product change or solving a key customer problem. Large companies such as Motorola, Ford, 3M, and General Electric, as well as many small and medium-sized organizations, have used cross-functional teams.

10.1.2 Effective Teams: According to Rensis Likert, organizations are best conceptualized by systems of interlocking groups connected by linking pins—individuals who occupy membership in two groups by being a boss in one group and a subordinate in another. Through these interlocking groups, the work of an organization gets done. Since individuals in organizations function not so much as individuals alone but as members of groups or teams, for an individual to function effectively, a prerequisite is that the team must function effectively. According to David Mc.Gregor, some of the characteristics of well-functioning, effective teams are as under:

1. The atmosphere tends to be relaxed, comfortable, and informal.
2. The group's task is well understood and accepted by the members.
3. Good communication and task-relevant discussion among the members.
4. Members express their feelings and ideas.
5. Conflict and disagreements are cantered around ideas and methods, not personalities and people.
6. When actions are decided upon, clear assignments are made and accepted by the members.

10.1.3 High-Performance Teams: These teams have the same characteristics but of a higher degree. According to Katzenbach and Smith, strong personal commitment to each other, commitment to others' growth and success distinguishes high-performance teams from effective teams. Teams and work groups are considered to be the fundamental units of organizations as well as the key leverage points for improving the functioning of organizations.

10.2 Exercise and Techniques Used in Team Building

A number of techniques and exercises are used in team building to facilitate team performance and to address specific problematic issues. They are useful and powerful ways to structure a team's activities and energies in order to achieve understanding of the issues and to take corrective actions. Team-building sessions often include many of the following techniques and exercises:

10.2.1 Interdependency Exercise: This is a useful intervention if team members have expressed a desire to improve cooperation among themselves and among their units. This exercise is also useful for assisting people in getting better acquainted, in surfacing problems that may be latent and not previously examined and in providing useful information about current challenges being faced in others' areas of responsibility. It works well with up to approximately ten people, but can become too cumbersome and time consuming if more than that number are involved. This exercise requires participants' cooperation and assumes no serious conflict situations. Serious intense conflict situations require a different structure and more time.

10.2.2 Appreciative Inquiry: This intervention was developed by Frank Barrett and David Cooperrider and refined by Gervase Bushe. This intervention is based on the assertion that the organization 'is a miracle to be embraced' rather than 'a problem to be solved'. The central interventions are interviews and then discussions in small groups or organization wide meetings. Questions include, 'what have been the peak moments in the life of this organization?' and 'what do staff members' value most about themselves, their tasks and the organization as a whole'? One of the important aspects that this approach seems to generate is more attention by the consultant and the client organization to the strengths of the organization and its members.

10.2.3 Responsibility Charting: This helps to clarify who is responsible for what on various decisions and actions. It is a simple, relevant and effective technique for improving team functioning. The first step is to construct a grid; the types of decisions and classes of actions that need to be taken in the total area of work under discussion are listed along the left-hand side of the grid, and the actors who might play some part in decision-making on those issues are identified across the top of the grid. Then the process is one of assigning a behaviour i.e. responsibility, approval required/right to veto, support and inform, to each of the actors opposite each of the issues. A fifth behaviour is non-involvement of a person with the decision; this is indicated on the chart with a dash (-). Responsibility charting is usually done in a work team context. Each decision or action is discussed and responsibility is assigned. Then approval veto, support and inform functions are assigned. This can quickly identify who is to do what on new decisions as well as help to pinpoint reasons why old decisions are not being accomplished as desired. It helps in improving the task performance of team work.

10.2.4 Process Consultation (PC): PC represents an

approach or a method for intervening in an ongoing system. Process consultation consists of many different interventions as it is not any single thing that a consultant does. The job of a process consultant is to help an organization solve its own problems by making it aware of the organizational processes, the consequences of these processes and the mechanism by which they can be changed. The PC consultant works with an organization, typically in work teams and helps them to develop the skills necessary to diagnose and solve the process problems that arise. Schein describes the kinds of interventions he believes the process consultant should make which include agenda-setting interventions, feedback of observations or other data, coaching or counselling of individuals and then give structural suggestions.

10.2.5 Role Negotiation: The first step in role negotiation is contract setting. Here, the consultant sets the climate and establishes the ground rules starting with what you want others to do more of or do better, to do less of or stop doing or remain unchanged. The next step is issue diagnosis. Individuals think about how their own effectiveness can be improved if others change their work behaviours. Then each person fills out an issue diagnosis form for every other person in the group. The next step is the influence trade or negotiation period, in which two individuals discuss the most important behaviour changes they want from the other and the changes they are willing to make themselves. Then the group breaks into negotiating pairs. When the negotiated agreements have been made and written down, the influence trade is concluded with a follow up meeting thereafter.

10.2.6 Role Analysis Technique: Role analysis technique (RAT) is used to help employees get a better grasp on their role in an organization. In the first step of a RAT intervention, people define perception of their role and contribution to the overall company effort in front of a group of co-workers. Group members then provide feedback to more clearly define the role. In the second phase, the individual and the group examine ways in which an employee relies on others in the company, and how they define his or her expectations. RAT interventions help people to reduce role confusion, which can either result in conflict or the perception that some people are not doing their job. A popular intervention similar to RAT is responsibility charting, which utilizes a matrix system to assign decision and task responsibilities.

10.2.7 Visioning: This is a term used for an intervention, in which, group members in one or more organizational groups, develop and describe their vision of what they want the organization to be like in the future. The time frame may be anywhere from six months to five years in the future. The concept of visioning is credited to Ronald Lippitt. It starts with writing down the characteristics they will like to see an organization having from one or two years in future. Characteristics are made visible on a flip chart paper and displayed, clarifications pertaining to the questions are made, subjects then extract themes from individual reports and report them to the total group. Visioning uses mental imagery or cognitive maps to describe an organization.

10.3 Team Building Interventions

Team building intervention can be defined as a process of getting either a new or poor performing group on track. Team interventions refer to entering into an ongoing system of relationships, to come between or among persons, groups, or objects for the purpose of helping them. Team building interventions play a vital role in organization development. Main team building interventions are discussed below:

10.3.1 Formal Group Diagnostic Meeting: The main aim of this meeting is to conduct a general analysis of the performance of a group i.e. to find out 'where the group is going' and 'how the members are doing' and to uncover and identify problems so that they may be worked on. This technique allows a work group to get away from the work itself to gather data about its current performance and to formulate plans for future actions. Formal group diagnostic meeting includes the following steps.

Preliminary meetings are held with the manager, team

members, and consultants if one is involved. In some specific cases, the specific agenda items are determined in these advance meetings so that team members have more time to prepare their thoughts for the diagnostic meeting.

A diagnostic team building meeting is typically one day in length. The meeting may be unfolded in the following manner:

1. The manager makes a few opening remarks, including an overview of the meeting, the purpose, ground rules, and roles. The manager then acts as a meeting facilitator or turns the time over to the consultant to facilitate meeting.
2. If it has not been done previously, the team is now given a flip chart and a few questions that are answered by the team, such as "what are the things we are doing well as a team etc."?
3. The team is given time to answer the questions. This can be done in any of several different ways.

   The total group can answer the questions together.

The group can be sub-divided into smaller groups to address the questions. The group can be divided into pairs to come up with answers. The group (or sub-groups/pairs) discusses the data clarifying, categorizing, and prioritizing the areas that need to be addressed.

The final step is to set up some plan of action to be taken to address the issues. This usually entails more extensive team building meeting(s) later on to resolve the issues.

At least one follow-up meeting is set up to bring closure if plans have not already been made to create action teams to address the issues. Several ways are available to make the diagnostic data public. These are as follows:

1. A total group discussion that involves everyone making individual contribution to the total assemblage.
2. Sub-grouping is another method, which involves breaking down the group into smaller groups in which more intensive discussions can take place and then the sub-groups report back to the larger group.
3. Another method is pairing of two individuals to discuss their

ideas with each other. Each pair then reports back to the total group.

After the data has been made public, the issues identified are discussed and are grouped in terms of the themes (say planning problems, interdepartmental problems, goal ambiguity problems etc.). Subsequently, an action plan is developed by the group. The primary objective of a formal group diagnostic meeting however is to bring to the surface problems and issues that need to be addressed. Taking specific action usually is reserved for subsequent meetings

The strengths of these interventions are: this is a good way to get everyone involved in the process of identifying what barriers are impeding the group's performance, to get an overview of the entire scope of problems with which the team may have to deal, and to lead up to a team building session. It is less risky, because the only thing is identifying the problems and making some recommendations on how to go about solving them. It is a good way to prepare for team building or other interventions that may require more personal energy, time, and maturity. The weaknesses include: first time around, this type of intervention may be overwhelming because there is a backlog of problems to deal with. For groups that do not have good processes in place to diagnose and address problems, this may figuratively open the floodgates. This is just the beginning of the process of problem solving for the team. There is still a lot of work ahead to achieve performance successes.

10.3.2 Formal Group Team Building Meeting: Formal group team building meeting occurs with a permanent work group, a management team, or a temporary project type team. It is one of the most widely used OD interventions. The main aim of this meeting is to improve team's effectiveness through better management of task demands, relationship demands, and group processes. Team development process involves helping the group learn to identify, diagnose, and solve problems with the help of an OD practitioner. The problem may involve the tasks or activities the group must perform; the process by which it accomplishes the tasks; or interpersonal conflict between two or more team members. According to French and Bell, team development is 'an inward look by the team at its own performance, behaviour, and culture for the purposes of dropping out dysfunctional behaviours and strengthening functional ones'.

The first intervention is to gather data through the use of questionnaires or, more commonly, through interviews. The nature of the data gathered varies, depending upon the purpose of the team building programme, the consultant's knowledge about the organization and its culture, other OD efforts taking place in an organization, and the people involved. The consultant already may have obtained a great deal of data by sitting in as a process observer at staff and other meetings. The data usually includes information on leadership styles and behaviour; goals, objectives, and decision-making processes; such variables of organizational culture as trust, communication patterns, and interpersonal relationships and processes; barriers to effective group functioning; and task and related technical problems.

In order to ensure that organization members have freedom of choice, the data gathering stage is initiated only after the manager and his group have agreed that team development is a process in which they wish to engage and have set of data for an off-site meeting. This happens frequently but not always and the data gathering stage is conducted as close to the actual meeting as possible. The off-site meeting may last from a day and half to a week, with the average being about three days. The meeting is held away from the organization to reduce the number of interruptions and other pressures that might inhibit the process.

When the meeting starts, the consultant feeds back the information that has been collected. This information usually is categorized by major themes. Based on his knowledge of the data and the group, the consultant helps in setting the agenda or acts solely as a process observer, feeding back to the group his observations of what the group is doing. The primary role of the consultant is to assist the group in learning to identify, diagnose and solve its own problems. According to Beer, the consultant can play several different roles during the team development meeting. One role is that of process consultant, helping the group to understand and diagnose its own group process. The consultant may also function as a resource person, offering expertise as a behavioural scientist, or as a teacher, giving information about areas such as group dynamics, conflict resolution, and leadership.

During the meeting, the group examines and discusses the issues, ranks them in order of their importance, examines the underlying dynamics of the problems, begins to work on solutions to the problems, and establishes some action steps to bring about the changes deemed desirable. It is necessary to have follow-up meetings to determine whether the action steps that were outlined were taken and to determine whether those steps had the desired effects. Generally, team building involves deciding on action steps for remedying problems and setting target dates for '*who will do what and when*'. A series of meetings is needed to ensure permanent change.

10.4 Manager's Role in Team Building

It is the manager who is responsible for group functioning, although this responsibility must be shared by the group itself. Hence, it is the task of the management to develop a work group, which should regularly analyze and diagnose its own effectiveness and work process. With the group's involvement, the manager must diagnose the group's effectiveness and take appropriate actions to eradicate operating difficulties or stress faced by the group. The issue of who should lead a team building session is a function of managerial capability, because many managers have not been well trained to handle the session.

The initial use of a consultant is advisable. The role of the consultant is to work closely with the manager and the members of the unit to a point at which the manager is capable of engaging in team development activities as a regular and ongoing part of overall managerial responsibilities. The two should work together as a team in developing the initial programme, keeping in mind that the manager ultimately is responsible for all team building activities, even though the consultant's resources are available and the consultant's presence is only to help the manager to learn to continue team development processes with minimum consultant help or without ongoing help of the consultant. Thus, initially the consultant might be much more active in data gathering, diagnosis, and action planning, particularly if a one-to three-day off-site workshop is considered. In later stages, the consultant takes a much less active role and the manager takes a more active role and serves as both manager and team developer.

10.4.1 Applicability of Team Building: Team building is applicable in a large number of situations, from starting a new team, to resolving conflicts among members, to revitalizing a complacent team. According to Lewis, the conditions best suited to team building are as under:

1. Pattern of communication and interaction are inadequate for good group functioning.
2. Group leaders desire an integrated team.
3. The group's task requires interaction among members.
4. The benefits outweigh the costs of team building.
5. Team building must be congruent with the leader's personal style and philosophy.

10.5 Inter-group Team Building Interventions

Richard Beckhard, an OD practitioner and one of the pioneers of OD, notes, "one of the major problems affecting organizational effectiveness is the amount of dysfunctional energy expended in inappropriate competitions and fighting between groups that should be collaborating". This competition and conflict is a result of varied objectives, values, efforts and interests of the two groups. The interdependence of functions is one of the potential sources of conflict.

10.5.1 Blake, Shepard and Mouton: This intervention is also known as confrontation. The concept was developed by Blake, Shepherd and Mouton. In this intervention, the consultant must intervene to open communication between two groups. It starts with inter-group team building meeting. This meeting involves the following steps.

1. Each group prepares the lists under the headings:
   - How do we see ourselves?
   - How do we think other department see us?
   - How do we see other departments?
2. Then the group meets and discusses the list with one of the team member as a spokesperson.
3. Then the group separately meets to discuss discrepancies and feedback. It allows correcting the perception and behaviours.
4. Cross groups are made with members from each department to diagnose the lists and develop a conflict reducing alternative. Together groups develop action plans for solving the problems.
5. A follow up meeting is scheduled to evaluate the progress.

10.6 Third Party Peacemaking Interventions

Third party peacemaking as the name suggests, focuses on the interventions by a third party to resolve conflicting situations. It is aimed at the analysis of involved processes, diagnosis of the conflict's causes and with the assistance of a third party, resolution of the conflict effectively. Richard Walton suggests that in third party peacemaking, the fundamental concept is that the consultant will make the two disagreeing parties to confront or to face up to the fact that a conflict does exist and it is impairing the effectiveness of both. The consultant will use the right intervention techniques for facilitating the significant issues involved in the conflict to surface. These techniques may be as under:

1. Wisely choosing the place.
2. Selecting proper environment.
3. Using effective intervention strategies.
4. Setting an appropriate agenda for the meeting.
5. Helping the parties in conflict to own up to their problems and find solutions.

Where the issues involved in the conflict are of a substantive nature, the peace maker will concentrate on the parties engaging in problem solving through rational bargaining behaviours. On the other hand, if the conflict is emotional in nature, the consultant might have to work hard at restructuring the perceptions and facilitate understanding between the parties involved.

10.6.1 Walton's Approach to Third Party Peacemaking: It has been devised by R.E Walton that a consultant is usually asked to help in resolving issues when two individuals who have critical functions in an organization are not working well together and are having major conflict or disagreement. Because the conflict has grown to a level where the two parties cannot remain objective enough to resolve the conflict themselves a third person or party becomes a mediator in the process to achieve resolution, who skilfully manages the issue. The basic steps in this is confrontation (the two parties must be willing to confront the fact that conflict exists and it has consequences for the effectiveness of the two parties involved), and diagnosis (the third party must be able to diagnose conflict situations). Walton presents a diagnostic model of interpersonal conflict based on four basic elements: the conflict issues, the precipitating circumstances, the conflict-relevant acts of principals and the consequences of conflict, and direct or indirect intervention by the third party in facilitating dialogue between the principals.

10.6.2 Advantages: These are as under:

1. In some cases, teams cannot progress because of the poor relationship between two key people. This is an excellent intervention to clear up key relationship prior to the entire team engaging in team building.
2. A win-win outcome leads to a tremendous release of positive energy toward productive gains, not just for the parties involved, but for all other co-workers as well.

10.6.3 Disadvantages: These are as follows:

1. The parties are sometimes not ready emotionally and mentally to resolve the issues and show counterproductive behaviours.
2. At times, the third party may be perceived as not being

objective enough or taking sides.

3. One or both of the parties may have a hidden agenda that throws the process off course and keeps it from being successful.

10.6.2 Role Negotiation Technique (RNT): It was developed by Roger Harrison in 1971 for improvement in the working of people and team. The technique rests on the basic assumption that most people prefer a fair negotiated settlement to a state of unresolved conflict, and they are willing to invest some time and make some concessions in order to achieve a solution. The process of RNT is as follows:

Contract Setting: Consultant sets the climate and establishes the ground rules. This step consists of individuals negotiating with each other to arrive at a written contract of what behaviours each will change.

Issue Diagnosis: Individuals think about how their own effectiveness can be improved if others change their work behaviours. Then each person fills out an issue diagnosis form for every other person in the group, where the individual states that he or she would like the other to do more of, do less of, or maintain unchanged, which then is exchanged among all members. The messages received by each person are written on a chalkboard or newsprint for all to see.

Influence Trade or Negotiation Period: Here, two individuals discuss the most important behaviour changes they want from the other and the changes they are willing to make themselves.

Role negotiation technique helps an organization in bringing about positive improvement in a situation where power and influence issues are working to maintain an unsatisfactory status quo. It improves team functioning.

Sometimes people are selfish and do not want to change their behaviour.

Points to Remember

1. A team is a small number of people with complementary

skills who are committed to a common cause, set of performance goals, and approach for which they hold themselves mutually accountable.

2. A work group is a group that interacts primarily to share information and to make decisions to help each group member perform within his or her area of responsibility. A work team is a group whose individual efforts result in a performance that is greater than the sum of individual inputs.
3. The main aim of the formal group diagnostic meeting is to conduct a general analysis of the performance of the group that is to find out 'where the group is going 'and 'how the members are doing' and to uncover and identify problems so that they may be worked on. This technique allows the work group to get away from the work itself to gather data about its current performance and to formulate plans for future action.
4. Role analysis technique (RAT) is used to help employees get a better grasp on their role in an organization.
5. Process consultation consists of many different interventions. The job of a process consultant is to help an organization solve its own problems by making it aware of organizational processes, the consequences of these processes and the mechanism by which they can be changed.
6. Third party peacemaking as the name suggests, focuses on the interventions by a third party to resolve the conflicting situations. It is aimed at the analysis of involved processes, diagnosis if the conflict's causes and with the assistance of a third party consultant, resolution of the conflict effectively.

Short Answer Type Questions

1. Define team.
2. What is the difference between effective and high performing teams?
3. Explain role negotiation.
4. Discuss the need of role analysis technique.
5. What is visioning?
6. What is process consultation?

Long Answer Type Questions

1. Why teams are important for the organizations? Explain the difference between group and team?
2. Define team interventions. Elaborate the exercise and techniques used in team interventions.
3. What do you mean by team? Discuss the various types of teams in detail.
4. Discuss various team interventions in detail?
5. What are the various exercises and teams used in team building?
6. Explain inter-group peacemaking interventions.
7. What do you mean by third party peacemaking interventions?

Multiple Choice Questions

Q. 1. Beckhard has listed how many assumptions about the nature and functioning of organizations

a. Six
b. Thirteen
c. Eight
d. Two

Q. 2. Quality circle is basically an idea based on

a. American synthesis on Japanese idea
b. Japanese synthesis of American idea
c. German synthesis on Japanese idea
d. American synthesis on German idea

Q. 3. Team interventions refer to

a. Learning incurred by the team
b. Helping members of the team to enhance performance
c. Eliminating differences within a team
d. Identify team's inter-personal skills

Q. 4. Team intervention can be useful for

a. Engaging and aligning team members to collaborate effectively

b. Bring a new idea within the team
c. Enhance organizational climate
d. Set clear standards for the team

Q. 5. Which of the following is not an area of team interventions?
a. Diagnosis
b. Task accomplishments
c. Empowerment
d. Team and organization processes

Q. 6. One common inter-group intervention is
a. Assessment
b. Role analysis
c. Probed protocol analysis
d. Conflict resolution meetings

Q. 7. Rotating membership intervention focuses on
a. Commenting on different group members
b. Minimizing negative effects of inter-group rivalry
c. Attitude correction of group members
d. Categorizing of group members

Q. 8. Third party is also called
a. Mediators
b. Moderators
c. Intermediaries
d. De-escalators

Q. 9. Walton's model on third party peace making is based on
a. Conflict issues
b. Personality issues
c. Performance gaps
d. Attitudinal measure

Q. 10. Walton's idea of productive confrontation is based upon
a. Exclusive positive motivation

b. Balance of power
c. Individual confrontation efforts
d. Optimum relaxation in the situation

Answer Key

Q.1.	A	Q.6.	D
Q.2.	B	Q.7.	B
Q.3.	B	Q.8.	C
Q.4.	A	Q.9.	A
Q.5.	C	Q.10.	B

11

Comprehensive Organizational Development (OD) Interventions

This chapter is focused on OD interventions that are comprehensive in terms of the extent to which the total organization is involved and the depth of cultural changes addressed.

11.1 Parallel Learning Structures

These are specially created organizational structures for planning and guiding change programmes. Dale and Zand introduced this concept in 1974 under the label *collateral organization* and defined it as "a supplemental organization coexisting with the usual, formal organization". The purpose of a collateral organization is to deal with "ill- structured" problems the formal organization is unable to resolve. Considerable experimentation with collateral organizations occurred in the 1970s and 1980s.

Bushe and Shani (1991) summarized and extended the work on this connection in their comprehensive treatment titled, "Parallel Learning Structures". Parallel learning structures are a mechanism to facilitate innovation in large bureaucratic organizations where the forces of inertia, hierarchical communication patterns and standard ways of addressing problems inhibit learning, innovation, and change. In essence, parallel structures are a vehicle for learning how to change the system, and then leading the change process. Bushe and Shani (1991) offered the term "parallel learning structures" as a generic label to cover interventions where: (a) a structure (that is, a specific division and coordination of labour) is created, (b) that operates 'parallel' (that is, tandem) with the formal hierarchy and structure and (c) has the purpose of increasing an organization's 'learning' (that is the creation and/or implementation of new thoughts and behaviours by employees)".

Parallel learning structure consists of a steering committee and a number of working groups that study what changes are needed, make recommendations for improvements, and monitoring the change efforts. One or more top executives should be members of the steering committee to give the parallel structure authority, legitimacy, and clout. Use is made of the facilitator role, data gathering, data feedback, and process consultation. Sometimes with the steering committee, other groups also exist. These are idea groups, action groups, or implementation groups. These groups serve specific functions designated by the steering committee.

A parallel structure should be a microcosm of the larger organization, that is, it should have representatives from all parts of the organization. Parallel structures help people break free of the normal constraints imposed by the organization, engage in genuine inquiry and experimentation, and initiate needed changes. They are a foundation of OD because they are prevalent in so many different OD programmes. The quality of work life programmes of the 1970s and 1980s used parallel structures comprising of union leaders, managers, and employees. Most socio-technical systems redesign efforts and open system planning programmes use parallel structures. High performance organizations often use parallel structures to coordinate self-directed teams.

11.2 Stream Analysis

This model was developed by Jerry Porras and is valuable to understand change and managing change process thoroughly. He classified organizational work setting (the environment in which people work) into four variables:

1. **Organizing Arrangements:** These include goals, strategies, systems policies and procedures.
2. **Technology:** It includes tools, equipment, machinery, work

flow design, technical systems.

3. **Social Factors:** These include culture, interaction, process, network attributes, and informal patterns.
4. **Physical Settings:** These include space configuration, ambience, and architectural design. The process starts with thorough diagnosis through interviews, brain storming sessions, and questionnaires. A task force of representatives from all parts of an organization reviews problems and categorizes these problems into four streams. Then interconnections between the problems are identified; more interconnections denote core problems. Action plans are developed which are various OD interventions based on core problems. Thus, OD interventions help to correct dysfunctional aspects and change job behaviour of employees and leads to organizational improvement.

11.3 Survey Feedback

An important and widely used intervention for organization development rests on the process of systematically collecting data about the system and feeding back the data for individuals and groups at all levels of the organization to analyze, interpret meanings, and design corrective action plans. These activities—which have two major components, the use of a climate or attitude survey and the use of feedback workshops—are called survey feedback. This approach is based on the Systems 1-4T 'management system'. Survey feedback has been recognized as a potential OD tool for a long time.

11.3.1 Steps of Survey Feedback: These are as under:

1. Organization members at the top of the hierarchy are involved in the preliminary planning.
2. Data is collected from all organization members.
3. Data is fed back to the top executive team and then down through the hierarchy in functional teams.
4. Each superior presides at a meeting with his/her subordinates in which the data is discussed and in which subordinates are asked to help interpret the data, plans are made for making

constructive changes, and plans are made for the introduction of the data at the next lower level.

5. Most feedback meetings include a consultant who has helped prepare the superiors for the meeting and who serves as a resource person.

11.3.2 Advantages of Survey Feedback: These are as follows:

1. Survey feedback has been shown to be an effective change technique in OD as it gets the entire unit/organization involved in the improvement process.
2. In a longitudinal study evaluating the effects of different change techniques in 23 different organizations, survey feedback was found to be most effective change strategy when compared with interpersonal process consultation, task process consultation, and laboratory training. It is a cost-effective means of implementing a comprehensive programme.
3. When everyone gets involved from the top to bottom, there can be an immediate and major impact on the performance of an organization.

11.3.3 Disadvantages of Survey Feedback: These are as under:

1. Managers and staff groups responsible for the survey feedback process may have difficulty reaching sufficient consensus about the purposes of survey, its content and how it will be fed back to the participants. Such confusion can lead to considerable disagreement over the data collected and paralyzes about doing anything with it.
2. High levels of distrust in an organization can render the survey feedback ineffective. Employees need to trust that their responses remain anonymous and that management is serious about sharing the data and solving problems jointly.
3. Most organizations have certain topics that they do not want examined. These can severely limit the scope of the survey process, particularly if the neglected topics are important to employees.

4. The survey feedback process can unduly disturb organizational functioning. Data collection and feedback typically infringe on employee work time. Moreover, administration of a survey can call attention to issues with which management is unwilling to deal, and can create unrealistic expectations about organizational improvement.

11.4 Large-scale Change and High Performance Systems

When a number of OD and other interventions are combined to create major changes in the total culture and operations of an organization, it is called large-scale system change. The creation of high performance systems, high performance organizations, high involvement organizations, or self designing organizations usually involves a broad array of interventions. It features extensive member participation and involvement. Changes in job design and workflow, staffing procedures, training, and compensation are usually combined with such interventions.

11.5 Trans-organizational Development

Trans-organizational development (TD) is seen by Cummings to be an important form of organizational change process for trans-organizational systems (TSs). Cummings has referred to groups of organizations that have joined together for a common purpose, including alliances and networks, as trans-organizational systems. TSs are functional social systems existing intermediately between single organizations on the one hand and societal systems on the other. These multi-organizational systems can make decisions and perform tasks on behalf of their member organizations, although members maintain their separate organizational identities and goals. This separation distinguishes TSs from mergers and acquisitions. As per Cummings (1993), there are following phases in typical TD practice:

1. **Identification:** This stage involves identifying potential member organizations best suited to achieve their collective objectives. TD practitioners assist early members in forming a steering committee, establishing criteria for membership,

and serving as brokers to introduce potential partners to each other.

2. **Convention:** Representatives from member organizations are brought together sometimes in a search conference, to assess the desirability and feasibility of creating a TS. These conferences permit members to share perceptions and ideas, to negotiate equitable benefits, and to develop action plans.
3. **Organization:** This involves developing the structures and mechanisms that promote communication and interaction among members that direct joint effort to the task in hand. TD practitioners help members create the roles, structures, and mechanisms needed to coordinate the collaborative efforts of the TS members. Practitioners need to play more of an activist role than is traditionally seen in OD. Also, it is required that practitioners should maintain a neutral role. They should not align with particular member organizations or people.
4. **Evaluation:** This involves assessing the performance outcomes, quality of interaction among the members, and satisfaction of members. Members need feedback so that they can identify problems and begin to resolve them. This is done by the interviews or survey of member organizations by change agents.

11.6 Beckhard's Confrontation Meeting

It is a one day meeting of the entire management of an organization in which they take a reading of their own organizational health. In a series of activities, the management group generates information about its major problems, analyzes the underlying causes, develop action plans to correct the problems, and set a schedule for completed remedial work. This intervention is appropriate where:

1. There is a need for the total management group to examine its own workings.
2. Very limited time is available for the activity.
3. Top management wishes to improve the conditions quickly.

4. There is enough cohesion in the top team to ensure follow-up.
5. There is real commitment to resolve the issues on the part of top management.
6. The organization is experiencing, or has recently experienced, some major changes.

11.6.1 Procedures to be followed in Beckhard's Confrontation Meeting: These are as under:

1. The meeting leader (usually someone from top management), begins the meeting, stating the goals and objectives. He also lays out ground rules, such as encouraging open discussion without fear of reprisal.
2. The large group is divided into smaller sub-groups of five to eight people with each group consisting of members from various parts of the organization. Top management is a separate sub-group.
3. For about one hour, the sub-groups identify the required things both personally and professionally to improve an organization's health. The list of items is summarized by each group on a flip chart, and someone from the group reports the results in the next session.
4. All the sub-groups reconvene into one large group and report back their list of problems and issues, with the meeting leader categorizes the lists into several major categories, followed by a break while time is taken to duplicate the lists for everyone at the meeting.
5. The larger group is divided into sub-groups composed of functional departments or area which is led by the functional manager of the area. Each group is given the following charges:

- Discussion of the problems and issues related to the area and prioritize them and determine the action plans.
- Identify and prioritize the problems and concerns of top management.
- Set up a plan to communicate and involve those members of the organization who are not present at the meeting.

6. The group reconvenes to report back to the main group their

answers and action plans.

7. The meeting leader and other top management give their initial reactions to the plans. They set up a follow-up meeting with the entire group.
8. Top management meets to set up plans of action to address the issues raised in the meeting. Functional groups also meet to ensure that follow-up action is being achieved.
9. Four to six week later, a follow-up meeting is held with the entire group to report progress on each action plan and to make course correction as needed.

11.6.2 Advantages of Beckhard's Confrontation Meeting: These are as under:

1. This is a quick way to improve an organization's health.
2. It improves communication at all levels of the organization.
3. It maximizes ownership and commitment to organization improvement.

11.6.3 Disadvantages of Beckhard's Confrontation Meeting: These are as follows:

1. This method backfires if plans are not carried out.
2. It is thwarted if top management does not support the process and follow up actions.
3. It may be hard and costly to get everyone together at the same time and place, if members are spread out geographically.

11.7 Strategic Management Activities

OD must develop outward-looking interventions directed towards environmental analysis and strategic planning to ensure that the organization is in synchronisation with its environment. According to Schendel and Hofer, strategic management process consists of six major tasks, which are goal formulation, environmental analysis, strategy formulation, strategy evaluation, strategy implementation, and strategic control. Several OD interventions directed toward strategic planning are goal setting activities, Beckhard's confrontation meeting, future search conferences, and phases 4, 5, and 6 of grid OD. Charles E.

Summer's strategic management activities consist of four questions;

1. What is your present strategy?
2. What are the opportunities and threats to that strategy?
3. What are your strengths and weakness to meet those threats and opportunities?
4. What kind of future policies you must adopt to avoid the threats and maximize your strengths?

A top management team works for six months to a year answering these four questions.

OD practitioners need to become experts in strategic management processes and need to have a through knowledge of strategic management content.

11.7.1 Real Time Strategic Change: It was devised by Robert Jacob. It is congruent with search conferences and strategic management activities. Some aspects of this intervention have been derived from the work of Ronald Lippitt. Real time is the simultaneous planning and implementation of individuals, groups, or organization wide changes.

A critical mass of organizational members, sometimes hundreds come together for a three day meeting to discuss organization wide issues. The assumptions underlying this event are as under:

1. A leadership team decides that its organization needs a new strategic direction based on drivers for change either from inside or outside their own organization;
2. A draft strategy is developed by a leadership team prior to the event;
3. The leadership group is open to feedback on the strategy by participants, and to revising it based on this feedback; and
4. The participants in this event comprise the entire organization, or a critical mass of people from a larger organization.

Jacob (1994) has described six key steps for developing a strategy:

- Identifying and clarifying the basic, important issues facing the organization as a whole.

- Agreeing on an overall purpose for the change effort.
- Deciding which people need to be involved in the change effort and how.
- Determining how much influence these people need to have over the development of this strategy.
- Clarifying the information people need to do quality work and make wise decisions regarding their collective future.
- Exploring the methods, processes, and approaches that boost people in making real time strategic changes.

The setting includes flip charts, break tables set with refreshment and snacks, and a podium and a microphone. While most of the participation is in small groups with maximum diversity of function and level (called max-mix groups), on the third day participants self-select themselves into action planning groups focusing on a sub-part of the overall strategy that is of most interest to them.

After that, participants work in their "back home" work groups for planning the next action steps. Throughout the process, participants are asked to react to material that has been generated by voting on items as "glads", "sads", and "mads", or posting gold stars or red rots. This process requires a great deal of planning and a great deal of facilitator assistance.

Extensive follow-up back on the job, or course, is essential. Implementation plans need to be made and leaders continuously heed to keep the broader system in mind so that plans and implementation occur both within and across the units.

11.8 Search Conferences and Future Search Conferences

Procedurally, these two interventions are same but different from each other due to their place of origin. Search conferences emerged with consulting practices in Great Britain, Europe, and Australia, while future search conferences emerged in United States. Merrelyn Emery and Ronald Purser in their book, "The Search Conference", distinguished between these interventions. According to them, the basic design of a search conference consists of three phases i.e. environmental appreciation (changes in the world around us and desirable and probable future), system analysis (history of the system, analysis of the present system, and desirable future for the system) and integration of system and environment (dealing with constraints and strategies and action plans).In the US, Marvin Weisbord has written extensively about future search conferences.

11.9 Managerial Grid

Robert R. Blake and Jane S. Mouton worked together at the Psychology Department of the University of Texas during 1950s and 1960s. They are known primarily for the development of 'Managerial Grid' as a framework for understanding managerial behaviour.

They subsequently set up a company, Scientific Methods Inc., to disseminate their ideas on organization development and management effectiveness.

Blake and Mouton set out to apply the ideas of behavioural scientists such as Rensis Likert to the practice of management. They built on studies conducted at Ohio State University and the University of Michigan in the 1940s which attempted to identify the behavioural characteristics of successful leaders.

Blake and Mouton identified two fundamental drivers of managerial behaviour as concern for getting the job done, and concern for the people doing the work.

They argued that, on the one hand, an exclusive concern for production at the expense of the needs of those engaged in production leads to dissatisfaction and conflict, thus adversely affecting performance, but that on the other hand, an excessive concern to avoid conflict and maintain good relationships is also detrimental to the achievement of goals and objectives.

In order to provide a framework for describing management behaviours, the two variables of 'concern for production' and 'concern for people' are plotted on a grid showing nine degrees of concern for each from 1 indicating a low level of concern, to 9 indicating a high level of concern.

11.10 Grid OD

While managerial grid is considered useful in helping managers to understand their own behaviour patterns it was recognized that only so much could be achieved through individual management development, and that problems are needed to be addressed at the work group and organizational level. Consequently, grid theory was used as a starting point for the development of organization development programmes designed to enhance managerial effectiveness, resolve conflict, and develop team work within the organization. The programmes follow a six phase approach:

1. Grid seminar.
2. Team development.
3. Inter-group development.
4. Goal setting and strategy development.
5. Implementation.
6. Stabilization.

A grid seminar generates awareness on how personal behaviours have an impact on others in the work place. Participants learn and practice specific skills in teams engaged in a structured critique that measures activity results at several levels. The skills are commonsense ones in any work place and include, for example, the best way to take initiative, resolve conflict, or make sound decisions. Participants use grid theory to clarify personal values and attitude regarding behaviour, and then work in teams to complete structured activities under time and performance pressure. The seminar is over 90 percent experimental, placing the responsibility for learning, practice, and change into the hands of the participants. This level of team involvement and responsibility is found to make the learning effective and lasting.

Phase 2 and phase 3 focuses on problem solving and conflict resolution, both within and between the work groups. A major concern is to enable the teams to develop the ability to work together towards a common goal in a synergistic way. In phase four, the focus moves to reaching agreement on broader, organization wide goals. Planned changes are implemented in phase five and in the final phase progress is monitored, to ensure that the changes continue in the work place, and are consolidated and stabilized. This programme is applied throughout the organization at all levels, and in large organizations, the process may take three to five years to complete. In the course of the programme, the focus moves from the behaviour of individual managers to the effectiveness of work groups and teams, and the involvement of the whole organization. For individuals, grid OD phase 1 is required.

Blake and Mouton also developed their own theories on how best to teach grid theories and concepts in the work group context. These are described in the book, "Synorgogy", published in 1984.The term synorgogy was coined by Blake and Mouton, and describes a systematic approach to learning that leads team members to learn from each other in a cooperative and participative way. Synorgogy is defined as working together for shared teaching.

Four synorgogic learning designs were developed to provide a structure for the process of learning. The "team effectiveness design" and the "team member teaching design" relate to the acquisition of knowledge. The "performance judging design" relates to the development of skills. Lastly the "clarifying attitude design" concerns awareness and development of appropriate attitudes. Techniques include implied individual preparation, presentations and multiple choices, and true/false tests and team discussion. The role of the learning administrator is limited to making sure that the learning design is effectively implemented. These methods were first used by Blake and Mouton to teach university courses but were later adopted to work place training sessions.

Points to be Remember

1. Parallel learning structures are a mechanism to facilitate innovation in large bureaucratic organizations where the forces of inertia, hierarchical communication patterns and

standard ways of addressing problems inhibit learning, innovation, and change.

2. Survey feedback has been recognized as a potential OD tool for a long time.
3. Stream analysis model was developed by Jerry Porras and is valuable to understand change and managing change process thoroughly.
4. When a number of OD and other interventions are combined to create major changes in the total culture and operations of an organization, it is called large-scale system change.
5. Beckhard's confrontation meeting is a one day meeting of the entire management of an organization in which they take a reading of their own organizational health.

Short Answer Type Questions

1. What do you mean by parallel learning structure?
2. What is high performance work system?
3. What is managerial grid?
4. What is survey feedback?

Long Answer Type Questions

1. Discuss the procedure to be followed in Beckhard's confrontation meeting.
2. Define trans-organizational development. What are the various phases of trans-organizational development?
3. Elaborate the variables used in stream analysis.

Multiple Choice Questions

Q. 1. The scope of comprehensive intervention is

a. Departments
b. Functional areas
c. Total organization
d. Representatives of top management

Q. 2. The first step in confrontation meeting is

a. Information collecting

b. Climate setting
c. Information sharing
d. Priority setting

Q. 3. Which of the following is not a type of structural intervention?
a. Management by wandering around
b. Self-managed teams
c. Management by objectives
d. Quality of work life projects

Q. 4. Work redesign is geared towards
a. How job affects attitude and behaviour at work?
b. Skill expertise
c. Task requirements of job holder
d. Supervisory support

Q. 5. Organizational development is best defined as
a. Intervened change
b. Systematic change
c. Flexible change
d. Planned change

Q. 6. People in an organization should be treated as
a. Important resource
b. Natural resource
c. Working capital
d. All of the above

Q. 7. Action research is based upon
a. Syllabus defined by a university for education purposes
b. Experimental methods suggested by the university
c. Studies carried on in an occupation, typically in education
d. Knowledge gained from corporate case studies

Q. 8. Action research is a_______type of process

a. Reflective
b. Proactive
c. Reactive
d. Operative

Q. 9. Action research involves
a. Career development
b. Participating in a change situation
c. Leading by role playing
d. Directing the managerial instructions

Q. 10. The term action research was termed by
a. Robert House
b. Kellogg
c. Kurt Lewin
d. Carl Rogers

Q. 11. "Organizational practitioner should consult the relevant employees". This is an example of which of the following contracting process
a. Describing
b. Mutual expectations
c. Time and resources
d. Ground rules

Q. 12. Which of the following is not a conflict controlling strategy?
a. Prevent the ignition of conflict
b. Set limits on the form of the conflict
c. Help the parties to ignore the conflict
d. Eliminate or to resolve the basic issues causing the conflict

Q. 13. Which of the following is not a part of team development in training meeting?
a. Norms of meeting
b. Setting objectives

c. Collecting data
d. Planning the meeting

Q. 14. A person who initiates, simulates, facilitates a change program is called
a. Organizational development manager
b. Organizational development practitioner
c. Organizational development stimulator
d. Organizational development facilitator

Q. 15. Which of the following models focuses on planned change as a cyclical process in which initial research about the organization provides information to guide subsequent action?
a. Action research model
b. Lewin's change model
c. Contemporary action research
d. Lickert scale

Q. 16. In IBM, some groups operate out of the human resources area and may report directly to the president of the organization. They can be categorised into which of the following OD consultant groups
a. Internal practitioners
b. External practitioners
c. Internal and external practitioners mix
d. General OD consultants

Q. 17. Culture reflects the values, ethics, beliefs, personality and traits of which of the following
a. The company's founders, management and employees
b. Management and customers
c. Just employees
d. The upper and middle management

Q. 18. Which of the following activities involves "motivating change" for effective change management?

a. Creating readiness for change
b. Describe the core ideology
c. Assessing change agent power
d. Activity planning

Q. 19. Which of the following stages may include installing new methods and procedures, reorganizing structures and work designs and reinforcing new behaviours in action research model?
a. Intervention
b. Planned change
c. Evaluation
d. Feedback

Q. 20. Which of the following is not a conflict controlling strategy?
a. Prevent the ignition of conflict
b. Set limits on the form of the conflict
c. Help the parties cope differently with the consequences of the Conflict
d. Highlighting the basic issues causing the conflict

Answer Key

Q.1.	C	Q.11.	C
Q.2.	B	Q.12.	C
Q.3.	A	Q.13.	A
Q.4.	A	Q.14.	C
Q.5.	D	Q.15.	A
Q.6.	A	Q.16.	A
Q.7.	C	Q.17.	A
Q.8.	A	Q.18.	A
Q.9.	B	Q.19.	A
Q.10.	C	Q.20.	D

12

Structural Interventions

The OD techniques discussed till now are behaviourist in nature. In addition to these, there are structural approaches also as a part of the OD programme. Structural interventions are also known as techno-structural interventions. Structural interventions refers to a shorthand term for a broad class of interventions or change efforts aimed at improving organizational effectiveness through change in task, structural, technological and goal processes in an organization. These interventions include changes in how the overall work of an organization is divided into units, who reports to whom, methods of control, the spatial arrangements of equipment and people, work flow arrangements, and changes in communications and authority.

12.1 Structural Interventions

Structural interventions that are frequently linked to organizational development are as under:

12.1.1 Quality Circle: Quality circles (QCs) are inherently problem solving and goal setting with an aim to enhance product quality. It originated as a Japanese management concept which was initiated by W. Edwards Deming, Joseph Juran and A.W. Feighenbaum. Quality circles consist of a group of seven to ten employees, across the units, who meet regularly to analyze and suggest quality improvement plans. These suggestions are forwarded to a steering committee for further action plan. The steering committee approves it and then action plan is implemented. The follow up meeting is conducted thereafter. Many organizations have implemented QC's successfully and achieved desired results. QC believes in continuous improvement by empowering teams.

12.1.2 Management by Objectives (MBO): Management

by objectives is a process of goal setting. It integrates individual goals with organizational goals. This approach includes improved performance, effective communication and participation which enhance morale and job satisfaction. MBO believes that if people are involved in setting goals, they will work harder and perform better. Participation in goal setting process allows managers to control and monitor performance by measuring performance and results as against two objectives which were decided by subordinates also.

12.1.3 Total Quality Management (TQM): TQM is a continuous quality improvement measure. It involves implementation of a number of organizational improvement techniques like quality circles, statistical quality control, statistical process control, self-managed teams, quality management systems and extensive use of employee participation. TQM and OD share common values i.e. system wide appearance that depends on planned change and belief in empowerment and involvement. It is found that TQM can be applied as one of the methodology along with other interventions for effective change efforts. Thus, TQM brings desirable benefits such as improved quality, higher productivity, and enhanced employee development.

12.1.4 Quality of Work Life (QWL): Quality of work life is considered to be a wide application of organizational improvement efforts. It attempts to restructure various dimensions of an organization. QWL is also characterized by employee participation. It also acts as a problem solving mechanism. QWL projects differ from organization to organization. But the features of QWL project remains constant.

12.1.5 Reengineering: Reengineering is also called as business process reengineering (BPR) which is a system wide change approach, focusing on basic processes of an organization. It can be defined as a fundamental rethinking or redesigning of processes to achieve improvement or change in performance. For successful implementation of BPR, it requires an effective team.

12.1.6 Learning Organization: It is a system wide change program that emphasizes on continuous self-directed learning that will lead to positive change and growth of an individual, team and organization. In the age of globalization, competition and new internet technology, organizations that are flexible and able to adapt according to challenges can sustain. Learning organizations are constantly responsive and can develop own technology or products according to changing competition.

12.2 Characteristics of a Learning Organization

1. Constant readiness for change and to take advantage of new opportunities.
2. Learning organizations have a continuous plan of integration of all levels within an organization.
3. Improvised implementation—learning organizations believe in experimentation rather than implementing rigid plans.
4. Collaboration and contribution by each level of an organization is crucial in a learning organization.
5. Commitment towards continuous learning is key element of a learning organization.
6. Continuous revaluation of various policies, procedures, plans is necessary for a learning organization.

12.2.1 Socio-technical System (STS): This theory was developed by Eric Trist, Fred Emery and others at the Tavistock Institute in the 1950s. According to this theory, organizations are comprised of two interdependent systems, a social system and a technical system. Any change in one system can affect the other system. To achieve high productivity and employee satisfaction, an organization must optimize both the systems.

12.2.2 Self-managed Work Teams: They are also alternatively called as self-regulating work groups, cross-functional teams, autonomous work groups, high performance teams etc. Self-managed work team is an autonomous group whose members decide how to handle and manage their tasks. The team comprises of members from different parts of an organization and with different skills and backgrounds. Top management gives authority to such teams for their group processes, structure of the team, requirements of the teams and objectives to achieve them. Diverse nature of teams helps in generating efficiency. There is increased responsibility on such teams as they have to set work schedules, prepare budget, create job assignments, develop performance goals, hire and select team members, assess the performance and have control on all group processes. Most companies may not use self-managed teams organization wide but they can be used for specific projects.

12.3 Characteristics of Self-managed Teams

1. Team members are committed to team and organizational vision.
2. Team members are highly skilled in their areas.
3. Information is openly shared.
4. High participation and empowerment is required.
5. There is clarity about roles in a team.
6. Decisions are made based on consensus.

12.3.1 Work Redesign: This model was developed by Richard Hackman and Greg Oldham. This model is an OD approach as it comprises of diagnosis, participation, and feedback and group development by redesigning jobs. The model recommends analyzing jobs using five core job characteristics which include skill variety, task identity, task significance, autonomy and feedback from job enhancing motivation, job satisfaction and work effectiveness. But some factors can minimize or moderate these outcomes. One such factor is knowledge and skill and deficiency in it can lead to less than the desired performance. Growth needs strength, is another factor. If this need is low i.e. individuals need to learn and develop can also lead to less motivation and job satisfaction. The third factor is 'context' satisfaction i.e. dissatisfaction with pay, job security, co-workers, and supervisors can also lead to less motivation. Thus, if the core job dimension is present in a job, the job characteristics model predicts certain positive effects in an employee's psychological state. This can thus lead to high individual and team development throughout the organization.

12.3.2 Survey Research and Feedback: Surveys are conducted for improvement. It is also considered as a communication tool. It helps to facilitate dialogue between employees and top management. Surveys help to assess the current state of an organization. It can also identify various problems that lead to less motivation or dissatisfaction. Survey research and feedback is a process in which OD consultant and members of an organization collaboratively collect the data and analyze them for proactive organizational change. With the involvement of top management, a preliminary planning of survey questionnaire is done. The survey questionnaire is then filled by organizational members. Data collected is summarized and fed back from top to lower level. Based on the feedback and problems diagnosed, an action plan is decided. This organization wide survey research helps to understand the problems and feedback which results in changes for desirable performance.

12.3.3 System 4 Management: This system wide intervention was designed by Rensis Likert. He identified four systems as follows:

1. System 1: Exploitative-Authoritative (autocratic, top down approach).
2. System 2: Benevolent-Authoritative (top down, less corrective).
3. System 3: Consultative.
4. System 4: Participative (based on participative methods of decision-making and supervision, emphasis on employee involvement and participation.) Likert devised a measurement device, i.e. questionnaire to indicate perceptions of employees of the organization which investigates the system 4 parameters. The results are plotted as a profile which illustrates difference that can occur in an organization to be least effective whereas system 4 connotes the organization being the most effective. OD practitioner must divert his/her efforts to move towards system 4 organization which can be done by involvement, participation and empowerment of employees.

12.3.4 Stream Analysis: The model was developed by Jerry Porras and is valuable to understand change and managing change process thoroughly. He classified organizational work setting (the environment in which people work) into four variables:

1. **Organizing Arrangements:** These include goals, strategies, system policies and procedures.
2. **Technology:** Tools, equipment, machinery, technical systems.
3. **Social Factors:** Includes culture, interaction, process, network attributes, and informal patterns.

Points to Remember

1. Structural interventions are also known as techno-structural interventions.
2. Structural interventions refers to a shorthand term for a broad class of interventions or change efforts aimed at improving organizational effectiveness through change in task, structural, technological and goal processes in an organization.
3. Quality circles consist of a group of seven to ten employees, across the units, who meet regularly to analyze and suggest quality improvement plans.
4. Management by objectives is a process of goal setting. It integrates individual goals with organizational goals.
5. Quality of work life is considered to be a wide application of organizational improvement efforts. It attempts to restructure various dimensions of an organization.
6. Reengineering is also known as business process reengineering which is a system wide change approach focusing on basic processes of an organization. It can be defined as a fundamental rethinking or redesigning of processes to achieve improvement or change in performance.
7. Learning organization is a system wide change program that emphasizes on continuous self-directed learning that will lead to positive change and growth of individuals, teams and

organizations.

8. Self-managed work team is an autonomous group whose members decide how to handle and manage their tasks. The team comprises of members from different parts of an organization and with different skills and backgrounds.

Short Answer Type Questions

1. Define structural interventions.
2. Explain the following terms:
a. MBO.
b. Quality circle.
c. Quality of work life.
d. Stream analysis.

Long Answer Type Questions

1. What are structural interventions? Discuss various structural interventions in detail.
2. Explain the characteristics of self-managed teams.
3. What are learning organizations? Why these are important?

Multiple Choice Questions

Q. 1. _______onsists of small group of employees who meet voluntarily to identify and solve productivity problem
a. Quality circle
b. Total quality management
c. Organization development
d. T-group

Q. 2. The inherent challenge of organizational development and change is
a. Retention of employees
b. Need to develop learning mechanisms
c. Maintaining a competitive advantage
d. None of the above

Q. 3. What makes change and planned change a way of survival?

a. The basic criteria of effectiveness
b. Adapting to new personnel
c. An ever-changing business environment
d. A change in the organization's status quo

Q. 4. What is usually the first thing an organizational development specialist does?
a. Select strategies
b. Diagnose system needs
c. Determine type of interventions
d. Interview top management

Q. 5. Reengineering, TQM and STS all acknowledge, in various ways, the importance of
a. Systematic investigation
b. Action research
c. Organizational learning
d. Energy and continuity

Answer Key

Q.1.	A
Q.2.	B
Q.3.	C
Q.4.	B
Q.5.	C

References

References

Athari, A.A. and M. Zairi (2002), "Training Evaluation: An Empirical Study in Kuwait", *Journal of European Industrial Training*, 26(5), 241-251.

Abella, Kay Tytler (1990), "Building Successful Training Program", Massachusetts: Addison-Wesley Publishing Company Inc.

Ackerman, L. (1985), "Development, Transition, or Transformation: The Question of Change in the Organization", Berkeley, CA: Being First, Inc.

Ahuja, K. (2006), "Personnel Management", 3rd edition, New Delhi: Kalyani Publishers.

Alliger, G.M. and E.A. Janak (1989), "Kirkpatrick's Levels of Training Criteria: Thirty Years Later", *Personnel Psychology*, 42(2), 331-342.

Armstrong, M. (1995), "A Handbook of Personnel Management Practices", London: Kogan Page Limited.

Aswathappa, K. (2000), "Human Resource and Personnel Management", New Delhi: Tata McGraw-Hill Publishing Company Limited.

Bartlett, K.R. (2001), "The Relationship between Development and Organizational Commitment: A Study in the Health Care Field", *Human Resource Development Quarterly*, 12, 335-352.

Bhatacharya, D.K. (2009), "Human Resource Development", First Edition, Mumbai: Himalaya Publishing House.

Brethower, K.S. (1967), "Maintenance Systems: The Neglected Half of Behaviour Change", in Rummler, Yaney and S. Schrader (eds.), 'Managing the Instructional Programming Effort', University of Michigan.

Brookfield, D. (1991), "Understanding and Facilitating Adult Learning: A Comprehensive Analysis of Principles and Effective Practices", San Francisco: Jossey-Bass.

Cook, S., S. Macaulay and H. Coldicott (2004), "Change Management Excellence: Using the Four Intelligences for Successful Organizational Change", London: Kogan Page.

Dawley, D.D., M.C. Andrews and N.S. Bucklew (2010), "Enhancing the Ties that Bind: Mentoring as a Moderator", *Career Development International*, 15(3).

Department of Finance (1995), "Introduction to Cost-Benefit Analysis for Program Managers", second edition, Canberra: AGPS.

Dwivedi, R.S. (2001), "Managing Human Resources: Personnel Management in Indian Enterprises", New Delhi: Galgotia Publishing Company.

Filipczak, B. (1996), "Who Owns Your OJT?", *Training*, December, 44-49.

Ford, J.K. and K. Kraiger (1995), "Application of Cognitive Constructs and Principles to the Instructional Systems Model of Training: Implications for Needs Assessment, Design, and Transfer", *International Review of Industrial and Organizational Psychology*, 10:1-48, Chichester, UK.

Gent, Michael J. and Gregory G. Dell'Omo (1989), "The Needs Assessment Solution", *Personnel Administrator*, July, 82-84.

Goldsmith, lrwin L. (1993), "Training in Organizations", Pacific Grove: Brooks-Cole.

Goldstein, I. (1993), "Training in Organizations: Needs Assessment, Development and Evaluation", Monterey, CA: Brooks-Cole.

Hamblin, A.C. (1974), "Evaluation and Control of Training", Maidenhead: McGraw-Hill.

Hashim, J. (2001), "Training Evaluation: Client's Role", *Journal of European Industrial Training*, 25(7), 374-397.

Holcomb, J. (1993), "Make Training worth Every Penny", Del Mar, CA: Wharton.

Howard, G.S., K.M. Ralph, N.A. Gulanick, S.E. Maxwell, Nance, S.W. and S.K. Gerber (1979), "Internal Invalidity in Pre-test, Post-test, Self-report Evaluations and a Re-evaluation of Retrospective Pre-tests", *Applied Psychological Measurement*, 3, 1-23.

Hunt, J.W. and Y. Baruch (2003), "Developing Top Managers: The Impact of Interpersonal Skills Training", *Journal of Management Development*, 22(8), 729-752.

Korner, S. (1986), "The Family Therapist as a Systems Therapist: Treating the Workplace", *Psychotherapy in Private Practice*, 4, 63-76.

Laird, Dugan (1978), "Approaches to Training and Development", Philippines: Addison-Wesley Publishing Co. Inc.

Lam, T.C. and P. Bengo (2003), "A Comparison of Three Retrospective Self-reporting Methods of Measuring Change in Instructional Practice", *American Journal of Evaluation*, 24(1), 65-80.

Lawson, K. (1998), "The Trainer's Handbook", San Francisco, CA:

Jossey-Bass.

Lee, P.C.B. (2003), "Going Beyond Career Plateau: Using Professional Plateau to Account for Work Outcomes", *Journal of Management Development*, 22(5/6), 538-551.

Lynton, Rolf P. and Udai Pareek (1978), "Training for Development", Connecticut: Kumarian Press.

Mamoria, C.B. (1995), "Personnel Management", Mumbai: Himalaya Publishing House.

Mathews, S. (1997), "Mentoring and Coaching: The Essential Leadership Skills", London: FT Pitman.

McGehee, W. and P.W. Thayer (1961), "Training in Business and Industry", New York: Wiley.

McGoldrick, M. (1985), "Genograms in Family Assessment", New York: Norton.

Nadler, L. (1984), "The Handbook of Human Resource Development", New York: John Wiley & Sons.

Nagar, V. (2009), "Measuring Training Effectiveness", *The Indian Journal of Commerce*, 62(4), 86-90.

Neo, E. (2000), "Human Resource Management: Gaining Competitive Advantage", 3rd edition Boston: McGraw-Hill.

Nisbett, R.E. and T.D. Wilson (1977), "Telling More Than We Can Know: Verbal Reports on Mental Processes", *Psychological Review*, 84(3), 231-259.

Noe, R.A. (2002), "Employee Training and Development", 2nd edition, N.Y.: McGraw-Hill.

Pace, W.R., S.C. Phillip, and M.E. Gordon (1991), "Human Resource Development: The Field", New Jersey: Prentice Hall.

Pattanayak, Biswajeet (1997), "Human Resource Training: Study on Training Need Assessment of Indian Industries", 1st Edition, New Delhi: S. Chand & Company Ltd.

Patton, M.Q. (1997), "Utilization-focused Evaluation: The New Century Text", Thousand Oaks, CA: Sage Publications.

Pearson, M.M., J.W. Barnes, and M.H. Onken (2006), "Development of a Computerized In-basket Exercise for the Classroom: A Sales Management Example", *Journal of Marketing Education*, 28(3), 227-236.

Prasad, L.M. (2005), "Human Resource Management", New Delhi: Sultan Chand & Sons.

Pigors, P. and A.C. Myers (1989), "Personnel Administration: A Point of View and Method", 9th edition, New York: McGraw Hill.

Quinlivan-Hall, D. and P. Renner (1994), "In Search of Solutions: 60 Ways to Guide your Problem-solving Group", San Diego, CA: Pfieffer and Company.

Robinson, D.G. and T.C. Robinson (1989), "Training for Impact: How to Link Training to Business Needs and Measure the Result", San Francisco: Jossey-Bass.

Romiszowski, A.J. (1993), "New Technologies in Education and Training", East Brunswick, NJ: Nichols.

Rossett, A. (1987), "Training Needs Assessment", Englewood Cliffs, NJ: Educational Technology Publications.

Rossi, P.H., H.E. Freeman and S.R. Wright (1979), "Evaluation: A Systematic Approach", Beverly Hills, CA: Sage Publications.

Rothwell, W.J., R. Sullivan and G.N. McLean (1995), "Practicing Organization Development", San Francisco: Jossey-Bass/Pfeiffer Publishers.

Rothwell, W.J. and H.C. Kazanas (1996), "Planned OJT is Productive OJT", *Training and Development Journal,* October, 53-56.

Santos, A. and M. Stuart (2003), "Employees Perceptions and Influence on Training Effectiveness", *Human Resource Management Journal*, 13(1), 27-45.

Schultz, Duane P. and Sydney Ellen Schultz (2010), "Psychology and Work Today: An Introduction to Industrial and Organizational Psychology", 10th edition, Upper Saddle River, N.J.: Prentice Hall.

Smith, A. (1990), "Evaluation of Management Training: Subjectivity and the Individual", *Journal of European Industrial Training*, 14(1).

Stanley, Llyod A. (1987), "Guide to Training Curriculum Development", Ljubljana: International Centre for Public Enterprises in Developing Countries, 118.

Storey, J. (1987), "New Perspectives on Human Resource Management", London: Routledge and Kegan Paul.

Swanson, RA. (2001), "Assessing the Financial Benefits of Human Resource Development", Cambridge, M.A: Perseus.

Swart, J., C. Mann, S. Brown and A. Price (2005), "Human Resource Development: Strategy and Tactics", Oxford: Elsevier Butterworth-Heinemann Publications.

Tai, W. T. (2006), "Effects of Training Framing, General Self-efficacy and Training Motivation on Trainees' Training Effectiveness", Emerald Group Publishers, 35(1), 51-65.

Thomas, N. Garavan, Carole Hogan, Amanda Cahir and O'Donnell Cork (2003), "Making Training and Development Work: A Best

Practice Guide", Oak Tree Press.

Tracey, W. (1984), "Designing Training and Development Systems", New York: AMACOM.

Vineyard, S. (1990), "The Great Trainer's Guide: How to Train (Almost) Anyone to do (Almost) Anything", Downers Grove, IL: Heritage Arts Publishing.

Warr, P., M. Bird and N. Rackcam (1978), "Evaluation of Management Training", London: Gower.

Watzlawick, P., J. Weakland and D. Jackson (1967), "Pragmatics of Human Communication", New York: Norton.

Worthen, B.R., and J.R. Sanders (1987), "Educational Evaluation", New York: Longman.

Worthen, B.R., J.R. Sanders, and J.L. Fitzpatrick (1997), "Program Evaluation: Alternative Approaches and Practice Guidelines", 2nd edition, New York: Longman.

Yin, R.K. (2002), "Case Study Research: Design and Methods, 3rd edition, Thousand Oaks, CA: Sage Publications.

Zemke, Ron and Thomas Kramlinger (1982), "Figuring Things Out: A Trainer's Guide to Needs and Task Analysis", Reading, MA: Addison-Wesley Publishing Company.

Index

Index